Feathered
Serpent
and Smoking
Mirror

Feathered Serpent and Smoking Mirror

C. A. Burland and Werner Forman

G. P. PUTNAM'S SONS · NEW YORK

Endpapers: Totonac relief of human sacrifice, from Tajin

Page one: Xolotl, the Evening Star, at the cross-roads of fate
(Codex Fejervary-Mayer)

Frontispiece: Tollan by moonlight

Page six: Teotihuacano clay mask of a vegetation god

© Orbis Publishing Limited, London 1975
SBN: 339-11609-5
Library of Congress Catalog Card Number: 75-15075
Printed in Italy by IGDA, Novara

Werner Forman and the publishers would like to acknowledge the help of the following museums and collectors in permitting the photography shown on the pages listed.

Biblioteca Universitaria, Bologna, Italy: 57 bottom, 100, 115.

British Museum, London, England: 34 top, 41, 42, 57 top, 61, 84, 85 top left, 85 top right, 87 bottom right, 88 top left, 88 bottom left, 94, 110, 114, 122, 123.

Philip Goldman, London, England: 72.

Hamburgisches Museum für Völkerkunde, Hamburg, Germany: 43, 56, 119.

Liverpool City Museum, Liverpool, England: 25, 28, 55, 65, 74-5, 95, 102.

Merrin, New York City, U.S.A.: 91, 99.

Museo de Antropologia de la Universidad Veracruzane, Jalapa, Mexico: 10, 11, 29, 50, 76, 104.

Museo Nacional de Antropologia, Mexico City, Mexico: 13, 16, 20, 21, 22, 23, 24, 31 bottom, 32, 36 bottom, 38, 40, 44, 45, 48 bottom, 63, 70, 75 bottom, 77, 82, 86, 87 left, 87 top right, 89, 93, 103.

Museo Nazionale Preistorico ed Etnografico Luigi Pigorini, Rome, Italy: 33, 37, 62, 64.

Museum für Völkerkunde und Schweizerisches Museum für Volkskunde Basel, Basel, Switzerland: 26, 59, 81, 83, 97, 101, 109.

Museum für Völkerkunde, Berlin, Germany: 35, 36 top, 48 top, 69, 73, 85 bottom, 88 right.

Museum für Völkerkunde, Vienna, Austria: 51, 54, 60, 90, 111, 112.

National Museum of Natural History, Smithsonian Institution, Washington D.C., U.S.A.: 34 bottom.

Portland Art Museum, Portland, Oregon, U.S.A.: 107.

Rassiga, New York City, U.S.A.: 9.

St. Louis Art Museum, St. Louis, Mo., U.S.A.: 49.

Contents

Foreword

Nothing in the long history of exploration, discovery and exploitation is comparable to the events leading to the destruction of ancient Mexican society in 1519. This was a head-on collision of two entirely separate worlds, both with equally long records of spectacular achievements, and yet both totally unaware of each other's existence.

A strange tale unfolds on the pages of this book: the Aztecs believed in and accepted the power of fate, but they did so because they had an unshakable faith in astrological computations and predictions furnished by their religious science. Stranger still, Montezuma seems to have possessed a detailed knowledge of the approaching catastrophe. While the motivations of his actions remain obscure, and so allow contradicting interpretations, there is no doubt that his assessment of the future was correct – the destruction was utterly inescapable.

WERNER FORMAN

Preface

A sense of fate overshadows Mexican history. The strange story of the conflict between the gods Feathered Serpent and Smoking Mirror largely determined the actions of the Aztec people when, in the early sixteenth century, the Spanish invaders brought the era of native rule to an end. At this point, history and mythology united for a moment to produce a great tragedy.

These two gods bore the Aztec names of Quetzalcoatl and Tezcatlipoca, and, like all Mexican deities, their names carried many metaphorical and symbolic meanings. Perhaps the best definition of their dual significance is psychological: Quetzalcoatl representing conscious intelligence and Tezcatlipoca representing the unconscious 'shadow' in the mind.

Though their technology was primitive, the Aztecs were no simple savages. Their great capital city of Tenochtitlan was built on islands at the centre of a lake, and became one of the largest cities in the contemporary world. Their orderly life allowed philosophers and poets to express and evolve a complex system of belief. They were deeply aware that life was transient within the apparent permanence of the world around them; their poetry likened the soul of man to a butterfly, coming to sip the nectar of a flower for a moment, and then passing out of sight. Their religion, however, based as it was on symbols of the forces of nature, included great cruelty and bloodshed.

The Aztecs believed that Quetzalcoatl would one day return to them from the exile forced upon him by Smoking Mirror, their war god and patron who had led them to the great victories through which they came to dominate Mexico. In 1519, strangers appeared on their shores, whom they believed to be the returning Quetzalcoatl. The date was the one predicted for the fulfilment of the ancient prophecy – the final and bloody confrontation between the Feathered Serpent and Smoking Mirror.

C. A. BURLAND

The Land between the Waters

Above: These pottery figures of two women with a man between them are typical of the western Mexican village cultures, the forerunners of the great Mexican societies. They were almost certainly intended to bring fertility

Left: After the fall of their great city Tollan, a few Toltec nobles escaped to preserve their heritage in the new city of Chichen Itzá which they built with Maya labour. Silhouetted against the morning sky are the serpent columns of the Temple of the Warriors, which once supported beams of carved and gilded cedar wood. Between them is the reclining figure of the rain spirit, representing a thunder cloud and carrying a bowl of water on his stomach which he will pour over the dry earth

Mexico was anciently known as Anahuac, which simply meant 'the land between the waters'. It is a mountainous country, set between the Caribbean Sea and the Pacific Ocean. In the west the Cordilleras form a part of the great chain of mountains which stretches from Alaska to Tierra del Fuego at the southern tip of the American continent. In Mexico the mountains divide, to enclose a high plateau where much of the history of the country developed, and in the heart of which Mexico City now stands. In ancient times the coastal regions were heavily forested, and the plateau was mostly grassland. The rivers were few and torrential, and the climate was steady, with a hot, wet summer, a short, cold winter and a sunny, dry season in the first quarter of the year.

The population of Mexico in ancient times was entirely American Indian. There were many different tribes, all tending to be brown skinned, rather small in stature, with brown eyes and straight, glossy, black hair. From the very beginnings there was a mixture of physical types among the Indians to the extent that some had a more massive build than others, and some had long skulls while others were broad-headed. These variations were not tribal, however; they occurred within every tribe, showing the racial complexity of the Indians as a whole.

The first Indians must have entered America via an ice-free but bitterly cold plain where the Bering Straits now bar the way. These people penetrated slowly southwards, hunting wild game and picking fruit. There is clear evidence that this began at least 27,000 years ago, and recent finds may indicate even earlier movements, as long as 50,000 years ago.

The key to the beginning of civilization was the discovery of agriculture. Just as tribes in ancient Iran discovered wheat and barley, so in northern Mexico the first maize was evidently discovered some seven or eight thousand years ago. Maize, which then bore only two seeds has, through human care, become the splendid plant bearing the large cobs which we know today. At that early time, tribes who developed a few maize patches in between periods of hunting had taken the first steps towards a new and more stable way of life.

The development of agricultural settlements in Mexico was slow, and there is evidence of village life only from about 1800 BC onwards. These early settlements consisted of nothing more than a few adobe huts clustered together. Even so, many very fine cooking bowls, carved in steatite, have been found on these sites by archaeologists. A few centuries later, however, pottery had taken over. All the villages made pottery figurines, probably for a fertility cult, and from these it is clear that women usually went naked apart from ornaments and body paint, while men tended to wear a loin-cloth. The staple food was maize, but additional sustenance from fruit and meat seems to have been easy to obtain. As villages on the high plateau as well as those from more distant sites all show considerable differences of style, it has to be assumed that, in the early centuries of its history, Mexico was populated by many small, diverse groups of people.

The most famous site of these village cultures was at Tlatilco, now on the outskirts of Mexico City. Here, among the local wares, another group of pottery figures emerges, representing humans with baby-like bodies and limbs. They are very finely made, and are related to the works of the so-called Olmecs. The matter of Olmec origins is still in dispute. On the whole it seems that Olmec-style rock sculptures at Chalcatzinco, on the edge of the high plateau, are earlier than the more famous sculptures from the Gulf Coast of Mexico. The major site for this culture is La Venta, in the state of Vera Cruz. There, typical relief carvings of the type developed at Chalcatzinco are to be found amid many monuments, including the oldest pyramid in Mexico. At La Venta, and at the nearby site of Tres Zapotes there were several gigantic heads which never had a body. Whether these helmeted heads represent planetary deities or not is a moot point, but they certainly represent a physical type still present in Mexico, with a high forehead, thick lips, flaring nostrils and straight hair.

The Olmecs were also masters of work in jade which they obtained from within their area of Mexico, showing a marked preference for the blue-grey varieties. The Olmec style is found in most areas of the country, though a green, crystalline stone was used in Oaxaca instead of jade.

The Olmecs seem to have been dispossessed in the fifth century BC, and Mexico was left without a highly developed culture for some three centuries, though village cultures continued to flourish and the arts became more advanced. What happened to the Olmecs is debatable. Art work resembling their style reappears in Oaxaca at Monte Alban in the second century BC,

and some of their symbols reappear in early forms of Maya and Zapotec writing, but their end remains as much an enigma as their beginnings.

In southern Mexico the Maya-speaking tribes were apparently living as primitive farmers, until their distinctive culture began to be formed in the first and second centuries BC. Maya art appears to have quite suddenly reached a high development in the second century AD. It is associated with pyramidal structures and the amazing invention, unique in the Americas, of syllabic writing. This remarkable people developed a civilization in which art tended towards realism and an almost baroque type of decoration based on plant motifs. It is interesting that among their sculptures we find analogues of the later Aztec deities, including Kukulcan who is equivalent to the god of the winds and the Morning Star who was later known to the Toltecs

Right: This massive head is one of several at La Venta, all equally mysterious. They may have been intended to represent planetary deities, but no explanation of their function is certain. They simply remain as splendid examples of the vigour of Olmec art. This art had great influence in later times, as is shown by the style of the carved boulder, above, from Jalapa in south-eastern Mexico. This shows a warrior carrying a shield and spear, with a war banner on his shoulder

Above: In the second century BC the people of Teotihuacan began to construct a great pyramid over a smaller one. This became the Pyramid of the Sun, one of the most enormous structures of the ancient world—three or four times larger than the great pyramid of Cheops in Egypt. This pyramid stood at one end of the 'Way of the Dead', a great avenue of ceremonial buildings which became the focus of the most influential city in Mexico. Even after the decay of their civilization, this centre had a profound and mysterious influence on the art and religions of later peoples. The Aztecs, for instance, believed this to be the birthplace of the present sun, which they thought of as the fifth that had been created

as Quetzalcoatl, the Feathered Serpent. In the same way, there was a black god Ek Chuah with similar properties to the Aztec Tezcatlipoca, the Smoking Mirror. These gods and several others seem to have been archetypal and deeply settled in the unconscious minds of most Mexican peoples.

In the tenth century AD Maya culture suffered a sudden and terrible collapse, when most of the ancient and beautiful cities they had built were abandoned. In later times, the Maya continued to live in a number of lesser city states, and subsisted on farming and fishing until the arrival of the Spanish conquerors. They lived for some time under the domination of the Toltecs who built, with Maya labour, the city of Chichen Itzá.

Living at the same time as the earlier phases of the Maya, and trading with them, were the Teotihuacanos of the high plateau of central Mexico. They are named after their capital city, about 20 miles north-east of

Mexico City. They appear to have begun as one of the more primitive farming peoples, but in the second century BC they began to cover a small temple-pyramid in their village with layer after layer of clay and rubble, facing the new and enormous construction with stone. This is now the gigantic Pyramid of the Sun. Leading to it they constructed a wide avenue flanked by smaller platforms. At the other end was another huge pyramid dedicated to the moon, and a great courtyard sacred to the winds and rain. This complex of sacred buildings was later surrounded by a city covering some eight square miles. The growth of this civilization is marked by an increase in the quality of pottery figures of the gods, and by the appearance of fresco painting. The culture of Teotihuacan is reflected all over Mexico and into Guatemala where, at Kaminaljuyu, a great city was built based on Teotihuacano culture but with close contacts with the Maya. Among the gods of

Top: This Teotihuacano-style stone carving from Xochicalco is in the form of a macaw. It is believed to have been used as a court marker in the 'sacred ball game', played throughout ancient Mexico. The players wore leather pads on their hips, falling onto their hands in order to swing this pad at a rubber ball which had to be kept in constant motion. Two teams played against each other, and it was believed that future events could be predicted from the progress of the game

Above: Clay mask of a god from Teotihuacan, which shows the typical facial adornment worn by the nobility of this society: a nose-pendant and large spools which hang from pierced ear-lobes

Teotihuacan the rain spirit, Tlaloc, was most important, but the Feathered Serpent, in his guise as a wind god, was prominent, and some of the deities show the dark face-paint later associated with the god of war, though he was not as yet distinguished as Smoking Mirror.

Teotihuacan flourished until about AD 650. It was destroyed by violence, but the great pyramids remained as a centre of pilgrimage through later ages. There can be little doubt that the Teotihuacanos laid the basis for Mexican highland civilization. They must also have inspired much of the artistic development of the Totonac peoples of the Gulf Coast of Mexico, who already foreshadowed much of later Aztec religion, especially in the sculptures of their sacred centre at Tajín.

A minor culture on the Pacific coast of Guatemala gains significance through the personalities of its gods. The Pipiles, as these people were called in later times, erected great stone stelae in their ceremonial centres, rather like the Maya, but the art style was more angular, and the symbols for dates were akin to those later used by the Aztecs. The great monuments, most of which are now in Berlin, show gods from the sky. Some reflect a great planetary serpent god, a form of Quetzalcoatl, and others show a war god who may be the early form of Tezcatlipoca. One stele from a site at Santa Lucia Cozumahualpa, represented a transit of Venus in AD 580, at a time when Teotihuacan was dominating most of Mexico. A century later this art style had infiltrated central Mexico and is found in the wonderful little temple at Xochicalco, which was without doubt dedicated to Quetzalcoatl. By this time Teotihuacan had fallen and that civilization had declined, though it survived in the smaller town of Azcapotzalco, where its styles amalgamated with stylistic influences from Guatemala.

Although it is clear now that the calendrical system used by the next dominant power in Mexico, the Toltecs, came from Guatemala, it is also clear, from native historical traditions, that there was an infiltration of tribes from the north. Certainly, the Toltec language, Nahuat, was related to the languages of some of the North American tribes. So it must be assumed that the Toltec culture had mixed origins. The costume and culture of the Toltecs, who established their centre in Tollan (now Tula, Hidalgo, a little more than 20 miles north of Mexico City) in the eighth century, was very similar to that of the later Aztecs.

With the Toltecs we enter recorded history, though it begins with the myth of the god Quetzalcoatl, who was sent by the supreme god to be an earthly king. This god-king went through a career as a good ruler, but fell victim to temptation by the witch goddess. He was intoxicated by the magic mushroom which she controlled, and in a euphoric daze had sexual intercourse with her. When he recovered he realized that he had broken the sacred traditions and must leave Mexico, taking with him his dwarfs, and other creatures, who all eventually died on the journey. This myth can be seen as an allegory of the disappearance of the stars and the planet Venus as they approached sunrise. When Quetzalcoatl reached the sea coast he embarked in a raft made of serpent skins and sailed towards the sunrise. He was absorbed in the fire of the rising sun, though his heart was seen shining in a solar eclipse. A picture of this event in an ancient Mexican sacred book, *Codex Vindobonensis Mexic. 1* now in Vienna, shows the eclipse with Venus still visible, and this astronomical event has been dated as July, AD 750.

After the ascent of Quetzalcoatl, history becomes clear, but the Toltecs, and all later peoples, remained sure that Quetzalcoatl was fated to return. The power behind the witch goddess was the demiurge Tezcatlipoca who, as the Blue Hummingbird, Huitzilopochtli, was to become the patron of the Aztecs. Tezcatlipoca was also well known among the Toltecs, and in the National Museum in Mexico City there is a carved frieze from an ancient Toltec temple situated on an island in the Lake of Mexico, which shows the figure of Tezcatlipoca complete with his symbol of the Smoking Mirror. Antagonism between the two gods, Feathered Serpent and Smoking Mirror, was already present in the minds of the Toltecs.

Above right: In the Toltec capital of Tollan (Tula) these columns, which stand 18 feet high, formed part of a great colonnade leading to the central pyramid. They are carved to represent the severe figures of Toltec warriors whose fighting prowess supported the Toltec empire. On their breasts they wore the firebird, symbol of the Toltec ruling class. Their head-dresses were made of shells and feathers, while their loin-cloths were tied with leather thongs

Bottom right: The three great empires of ancient Mexico were all centred around capital cities situated on the central plateau. The first, Teotihuacan (200BC–AD650) seems to have been more a cultural centre than an imperial city, but the Toltecs (AD750–1000) formed a great empire based on their capital, Tollan, now called Tula. The Aztec empire, which lasted from about 1325 until the fall of Mexico in 1521, was the greatest in extent and influence. Its centre was the great city of Tenochtitlan, built on islands at the centre of the Lake of the Moon. Although the city was destroyed by the Spanish invaders, Mexico City, the capital of modern Mexico, grew on the same site

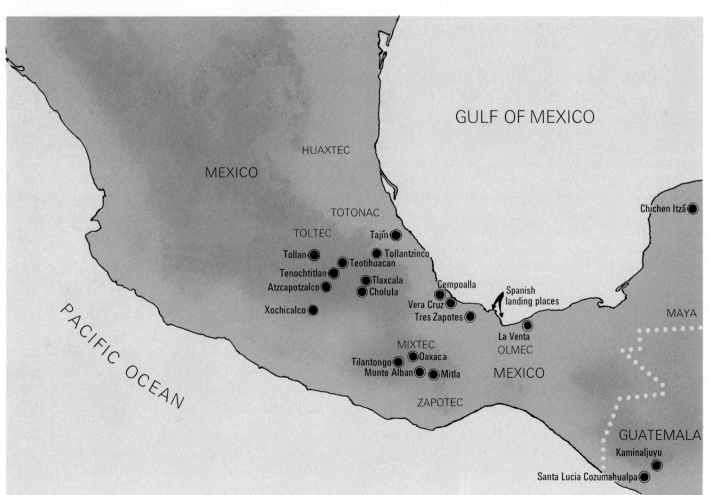

Above: Two Totonac stone carvings from Tajín. Small carvings of this type, called palmas, *were probably part of the ceremonial adornment of priests, but may have been used during the 'sacred ball game'. The figure on the left, probably a deity, is holding a rope attached to the column behind him. The column is decorated with double scroll patterns, typical of Totonac decoration. The figure on the right represents a prisoner with his hands bound behind him, ready for sacrifice*

There were nine Toltec kings, each of whom bore the title of Quetzalcoatl, though their personal names were often different. The *Codex Vindobonensis Mexic. 1* records their major activities very concisely. Then, in about 990, the Toltec Empire collapsed. A dynastic dispute arose because the last king Quetzalcoatl of the Toltecs married a woman of low social class, who was not descended from the house of the first Quetzalcoatl. The disputes led to a bitter civil war in which Tollan was left a desolate ruin. Some descendants of the Toltec royal family, led by another Quetzalcoatl, entered Yucatan and fought their way northwards. With Maya labour they established a new city at Chichen Itzá which reproduced many of the glories of their lost home. Later they lost power, and only his title as ruler remained to their leader, the Tutul Xiuh, the Firebird, who was left with no real command over the many contentious groups of the late Maya period.

The Toltecs had ruled most of Mexico from their centre of Tollan, but the story of the collapse of their 'empire' suggests that it had been an enforced system of tribute-paying states similar to the later Aztec system.

In south-western Mexico, the Zapotec kingdom lasted through many historical periods. The Zapotecs had succeeded other peoples in the same area, who had preserved some echoes of Olmec culture in their carvings, now known as *Los Danzantes,* in Monte Alban. They established a divine kingship which ruled from Monte Alban and later from Mitla in the State of Oaxaca. From the second century AD until about 1480 their rule ran almost unchanged. The pottery displays a unity of type, with slight variations as the balance of Mexican culture changed. The gods of the Zapotecs differed somewhat from those of the Toltecs, and their calendrical symbols were entirely different. They seem to have been an independent people with little wish to extend their territory. On their borders to the north, in the States of Nayárit and Colíma, there were people who continued the traditions of the ancient village cultures of Mexico in isolation. Their great period as artists was from the fifth to the seventh century AD, but they had no writing, and therefore no written history.

In the mountains of Oaxaca, the Mixtecs lived above the Zapotecs. A highly cultured people, they spoke a language related to Zapotec. They were fine craftsmen in lapidary work, gold and painting, but as they were unable to subdue their inter-tribal jealousies, they were usually only a loose confederation of small towns. In the eleventh century, however, a great warrior chief, Eight Deer Ocelot Claw, came to power in Tilantongo and succeeded in uniting them to such an extent that they defeated the Zapotecs and conquered the sacred towns of Monte Alban and Mitla. After his death, however, there was a return to the *status quo.* The most beautiful of all the surviving Mexican history books, *Codex Zouche-Nuttall,* now in the British Museum, deals with this period in detail, and also gives a general history of some other Mixtec tribes. In particular it is devoted to the ruling family of Tilantongo.

The Mixtecs had a great influence upon the arts of Mexico from the eleventh century. They claimed descent from the great Toltec rulers, and their artists were much in demand among other tribes, particularly, in later times, among the Aztecs.

Both Mixtecs and Zapotecs were overthrown by the Aztecs in the late fifteenth century. Three Mixtec tribes lost the whole of their manpower as sacrificial victims for the dedications of the great temple in Tenochtitlan, now Mexico City, under the Aztec Great Speaker Ahuizotl. But, until that horrific event, the Mixtecs continued to live in their independent mountain villages in a more or less peaceful way.

It has become obvious that Mexican history, even

Below: This wall stood in front of the main pyramid in Tollan (Tula) and has been partially restored. It served to delineate the holy area into which only nobles and officiating priests were allowed. The patterns running along the top of the wall symbolize the clouds over Mexico. The two outer bands of relief carving below are decorated with quadrate designs representing the earth, and between them the wider band contains representations of feathered serpents and skulls. The wall was once painted in brilliant colours, with the lower part stuccoed, and the overall effect must have been very dramatic

when it becomes documented, is a chronicle of tribal movements, which only becomes a record of Mexico as a large civilized area at three distinct times. These were the growth of the Teotihuacano culture, the spread of the Toltec hegemony, and, finally, the rise of the Aztecs. On balance it seems that all three centralizing cultures were militaristic and predatory, forcing the payment of tribute in goods to the central authority. As each civilization collapsed it was followed by a period of anarchy. The last period after the collapse of the Toltec hegemony was the longest, lasting for three centuries.

During the interregnum, after the destruction of Tollan, the country was in a state of confusion. The techniques of civilized living were not lost, but there had been terrible destruction and depopulation after the civil war. The traditions tell of plagues caused by thousands of dead bodies rotting in the fields. The

Right: In the heart of the great city of Chichen Itzá, founded by refugee Toltec nobles, stood this great pyramid dedicated to Quetzalcoatl. At the top a god-house has been reconstructed which faces the four directions. In a Toltec temple dedicated to Quetzalcoatl there would have been no human sacrifice, simply offerings of fruit and flowers. On the left is the lone figure of a standard bearer. The pole he once held in his outstretched arms bore great discs and streamers composed of beautiful feather work. On his back is a decorated shield typical of the Toltec warrior

population was faced in addition with famine because agriculture was disrupted. In the thirteenth century, it became important for the Aztecs to acquire a Toltec bride for their war-leader so that his sons should inherit the right to rule as descendants of the Toltec Quetzalcoatl. They could find only eight families of true Toltec descent in the country.

There were many attempts by city states to form small 'empires'. One of the first examples must have been the power exerted by Eight Deer Ocelot Claw. Another Mixtec tribe depicted the beginnings of its history in the Selden Roll which is now in the Bodleian Library at Oxford. They tell of their supplication to Quetzalcoatl, and of a pilgrimage which resulted in finding a temple of the priests of Quetzalcoatl. From there they were sent on another pilgrimage, and as they marched, they crossed a stream beside which they found an ancient figure of the god, which they then carried with them. A dark war god was also given to them as a guardian, and they eventually reached a mountain where they fought to capture a town, where they then erected a temple for each of the two gods. Then, with the blessings of Quetzalcoatl they conquered four other tribes. Here our knowledge of the painted story ends; the rest of the document was lost long before John Selden gave it to the University in the early seventeenth century.

In the twelfth and thirteenth centuries, the whole of Mexico was made up of small groupings of tribal societies, in which some towns had dominion over their neighbours. The pattern was not stable, as there were continual revolts in which the master might become the tribute payer at almost any time. There was no great decline in arts and crafts, and the temple priests continued to feed the gods with human sacrifice. Most of the hearts torn from the breasts of the victims were offered to the great Smoking Mirror, but there were also a few temples in which Quetzalcoatl was remembered, the god whose name is often translated as the

Feathered Serpent, and who demanded no sacrifice except of fruit and flowers.

The position was complicated by a steady intrusion of tribes from the north, the Chichimeca. They were usually barbarous and warlike tribes fleeing from the great droughts which had begun to destroy the plantations and shrink the rivers in North America. The Chichimeca learned the arts of Mexican civilization and many of their chiefs became notable rulers of more ancient cities. It is possible that the Aztecs descended from a similar more northerly group, but they began as a small and poor tribe. Their story begins in the year 1168, with a series of adventures which are almost exactly like the story painted in the Selden Roll. The third Aztec Great Speaker had history re-written, and so the narrative, in its first stages at least, is not truly history. Rather it is a revision of a much more generalized migration legend. There is reason to believe

the latter part of the story, however, which tells how they escaped from bondage under the Chief Coxcoxtli of Colhuacan and were forced to take refuge on islets and rocks in the great Lake of the Moon. There they built their great city, Tenochtitlan.

The whole of Aztec history reflects the people's dependence on the tribal god Huitzilopochtli, Blue Hummingbird, who was a form of Smoking Mirror. From the very beginning they were a dedicated people, and their leaders and prophets were always aware that they would achieve greatness and come to rule all Anahuac. But they also knew that one day the power of their patron god would be overthrown and that Quetzalcoatl, the god of the Toltecs, would return to bring a new kind of life to them. That is indeed what could be said to have happened, though through the agency of strange men from another continent of which the Aztecs could have had no knowledge.

The Gods of Mexico

Above: The rattlesnake, as is shown by this beautifully carved and polished diorite figure, was held in almost affectionate veneration, because of its links with the earth and the underworld

Left: The almost spectral figure of the death goddess Mictlantecihuatl, consort to the Lord of the Dead. Like all the gods of the Aztec pantheon, she is surrounded by a system of symbols bound up with the calendrical system and the poetic language of Nahuatl, which is full of metaphor and allusion. This leads to a great complexity, where each god or goddess may have many aspects and where some gods become merely aspects of others. In this case the death goddess is shown girded by a skirt of rattlesnakes, which were regarded as symbols of the underworld because they crawled from holes in the ground

A casual acquaintance with Aztec ideas of religion gives an immediate impression that the gods were figures from a wild, undisciplined nightmare. Further study, however, shows that this was not the case. The festivals of the Mexican year were arranged in a sequence which reflected the agricultural life of a nation—from seed-time to harvest and winter storage. In addition, an interleaved system of ceremonies was dedicated mainly to the war gods, as patron spirits of the nation. This dualism in religious outlook was reflected on the great temple pyramid in the heart of Tenochtitlan, now Mexico City. On the very top of the building was a double temple, one half of which was dedicated to Huitzilopochtli, the war god, and the other to Tlaloc, the rain god. This emphasized both the dependence of the Mexicans upon the forces of nature and the warlike spirit of their young men.

On the whole, Aztec culture was remarkably close to North American Indian ways of life. The worship of the corn spirits was fundamental, because it brought food, and was associated with fertility. And in a tribal situation, with the possibility of conflict with one's neighbours ever present, it was also necessary to placate the spirits of war.

Aztec social organization was basically agricultural. The people clustered around a town, each family working a plot of land. In more advanced conditions the system changed to include dominion by one group over other tribes, and the payment of tribute to the overlords. Even the highest dignitaries of state, however, had to take part in ceremonies of planting and reaping the corn, since the main purpose of Aztec religion was to keep the people in good health, with plenty of food, and a full enjoyment of the benefits of life, by placating the hierarchy of gods with continuous sacrificial offerings.

The war cults occupied a specified period of life in which young men left their families at the age of 17 or

18, and spent some three to five years in military service. Normally they returned to civilian life at the end of their period with the army. But in times of war every male under about 40 was likely to be called on to join battle with the enemy.

A diagram of the Mexican calendar in relation to the particular gods would show that 18 periods of 20 days each fall under a very definite series of protectors and this system of patron deities of time extends to all other methods of time counting. There were patron gods of the years, decided by the day on which each year could open. There were patron gods of the nights, which appeared in an ever recurring system of 13 deities, known as Lords of the Night. They represented the fate of individual nights, from the beginning of the calendrical day, at sunset, until the sun rose in the morning. Days were given names, not in a series of seven, as in our own calendar, but in a series of 20

named days. Each of these days had its patron deity, so that there was a constant progression of gods, who in turn looked after all the days and all the nights.

The codices

The extraordinary gods of the ancient Mexicans can be seen painted in the sacred books, which we know as the codices. The Mexicans called them 'thought paintings', which expressed their function well. They do not represent words, because there were so many different tribal languages spoken in ancient Mexico that it was actually more practical to read pictures than to try to create an alphabetic or syllabic system of writing. The gods appear very sharply as mysterious but strangely attractive figures. They are presented with the head in profile, the body directly facing the viewer and the feet also in profile. The hands are shown directly facing the

viewer, and, by their positions, the actions they are performing can be judged. The basic distinguishing characters of the gods are to be seen in their face paint as well as in the ornaments that they wear.

The codices are books made of fine strips of deer skin, usually about seven or eight inches in width, and about four feet in length. These skins were carefully scraped and cleaned, smoked over a slow fire, scraped again, softened, and well beaten, so that the leather became as soft and flexible as, say, a North American Indian's pair of leggings. Leather in this soft state was then painted over with a paste of limewash. The lime seems to have come from many different kinds of stone or from shell—in fact, from whatever was locally available. It was very carefully applied in a thin, even coat, less than a millimetre in thickness.

When the lime had dried, the Tlacuilo, or 'putter down of thoughts', planned out his series of pictures.

One occasionally finds traces of ruled lines, very thinly inscribed in red, which mark out the proportions of the figures to be painted on the pages. When the figures were satisfactory, the main colours were painted in. These colours were never mixed, and there was no shading in any of the pictures. Red was made from cochineal; green was sometimes a deep green from a vegetable dye, which has since faded to a golden-brown colour, though there was also a mineral green; blue was usually made from a special clay, but sometimes from chalk which had been dyed with flower petals. Yellow and orange were mineral colours, and occasionally small areas of purple were obtained from a shellfish, found off the coast of Oaxaca. This is almost identical to the murex from which Tyrian purple used to be extracted in the ancient Mediterranean. When the painting was dry the artist went round all the outlines of the figures with black, normally using a kind of reed

pen. The lines are very precise, of even width, and the whole picture becomes an accurate and strong statement in brilliant colours, framed within these black outlines.

The page itself has a very pleasing appearance with a white background on which the coloured figures are displayed in fairly open, rhythmic structures. Divisions in the text are marked by red cochineal lines crossing the page. When all this work had been painted on the long strip of prepared skin, the artist then cut into the limewashed surface, probably with a bone scriber, making vertical incisions at regular intervals, so that the long strip could be folded like a fire screen. The strips are of varied lengths, because there was no limit to the number of shorter strips which could be joined together to make a very long document. Indeed, some of these documents are over 20 feet in length. They fold up and appear to be like books, but the pages are not separate,

and the whole strip is painted on both sides. After reading one side, the codex can be folded, turned over, and opened again, so that the other side is ready for inspection. At the ends of each side, firmer pieces, either of leather or of board, were pasted on, and these served as protective surfaces.

Some of the documents are historical, but the majority are religious, and it is from these that we can see the images of the gods, and count the rhythm of time. But we would now be unable to make any sense of the codices, were it not for the work of the devoted Franciscan Father, Bernardino de Sahagún, shortly after the fall of the Aztec empire. From his church in Tlaltelolco, a part of modern Mexico City, he invited his pupils, the sons and grandsons of Aztec noblemen, to bring him accounts of life in ancient times. It seems that the elders responded nobly, because in almost the whole of his work, and certainly in the calendrical portion, there is only one mistake in the name of the god associated with a time period.

From the religious manuscripts, our knowledge extends to the meaning of the sacred figures and ceremonial masks which have survived from ancient Mexico. There is a strange quality about this surviving art, which is not unlike the quality of the country. It is strong and often savage; it reflects the quality of the thunderstorm amid the mountains, of the occasional floods which spread over the plains, and of that mysterious sadness which comes from visiting the sites of vanished civilizations. This is particularly strong in the case of the great Toltec capital of Tollan, now a cluster of broken walls and torn pyramids in the midst of a dusty desert. One can almost feel the terrible struggle which was said to have taken place between the devotees of Huitzilopochtli and those of the beloved Quetzalcoatl, who was the father of the Toltec empire.

Aztec cosmology

To understand the nature of their extraordinary religion, we must try to grasp the world plan which the Aztecs had in mind. It was based on the assumption that the earth was more or less flat. Aztecs had no idea that they were standing upon a spinning sphere, gyrating around the sun. Instead, they believed that above the waters and the underworld, a flat earth stood in a great ocean, which extended to the edges of the dome of the sky. Above the earth there were several layers of sky, in which the planets and the starry globe of heaven slowly revolved. There was also a mysterious point which never moved—the area near the Pole Star, which was thought to be an extension into an unknown universe, wherein lived the power above. This power was thought to be at once male and female and was called the Two Lord, Ometecuhtli. His temple was the whole universe, and it was said by philosophers

that he sat alone. In his hands he held a drop of water, and in this drop of water, there was a single green seed; this tiny seed was the whole of our world immersed in the ocean.

This concept was reflected in the fact that on earth no temple was erected to Ometecuhtli. His sacred place was in the hearth, in the middle of each household, where the fire was also worshipped as a god, symbolizing the life of the divine being who was in the centre of all things, and in the heart of all people. He it was who fertilized the womb, and gave life to the forthcoming child. This theology reflects the facts of normal life, since no matter how much sexual intercourse took place in the family, pregnancy only rarely occurred. The Mexicans interpreted this as the giving of life directly from the creator.

It was very important to the Aztecs, as well as to most North American Indians, to have a knowledge of the four directions of this world. They were: the east, where the sun rose; the south, where the sun was highest in the sky; the west, where the sun set; and the north, where the sun was never visible. These four directions were the keys to an understanding of all religious and magical thinking.

This sequence of the path of the sun through the sky and into the underworld was also the sequence of life, in which the human being rises, becomes vigorous, weakens, and dies. The concept of growth and decay was essential, and it was linked with the idea of the sequence of the seasons and of the hours. It also had obvious affinities with the life of vegetation. A picture in *Codex Fejervary-Mayer*, now in Liverpool, shows that the east was the home of the Morning Star, the south the home of the Mother Earth, the west the home of the Lord of Jewels, and the north the land of the dead, as well as the land of the maize seed, which was conceived

27

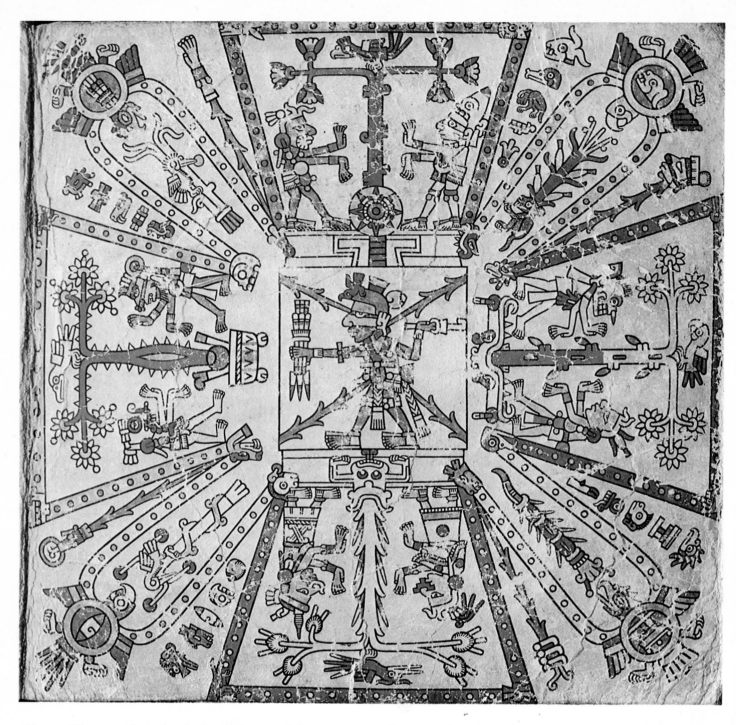

Above: This page from the Codex Fejervary-Mayer *shows the fire god at the centre of the universe being fed on the blood of sacrifice which emanates from the head, hand, leg and ribs of the god Tezcatlipoca (placed just clock-wise of each diagonal). The design shows clearly the great importance to the Aztecs, as to all American Indians, of the four directions. Each direction is represented by a tree on top of which is a bird, the tree being supported by the two gods associated with that direction. The northern direction, for example, which is to the right of the page, shows a tree laden with the stone knives of sacrifice growing from the open jaws of the earth. The two gods are Mictlantecuhtli, Lord of the Dead, and Cinteotl, the maize goddess. In the four corners, besides the dismembered Tezcatlipoca, are date symbols*

of as dead maize, awaiting its resurrection in the morning of the year.

There was a reflection of this progression in the circle of the heavens. The Aztec deities could be found in the stars, where they had their dwelling houses in the signs of the zodiac. It is especially interesting to note here that many of these star groups were given names similar to those in use in Europe and Asia. That there was any very ancient cultural contact which may have determined this is by no means sure. It may be that the association of groups of stars with the symbols gave rise to some similar names, not only because of the shape of the groups, but also through associations with fertility in the form of seasonal growth and decay.

Another remarkable coincidence is that the Mexicans

began their account of time (not the year but the circuit of 52 years, which was their basic time count) with the appearance of the stars of the Pleiades on the eastern horizon at sunset. This occurs early in November, and it links with the basic calendar of ancient Europe, in particular the one used among the Celtic peoples. The Celts held their ancient fire festival celebrating the setting of the sun, and, of course, expressing the hope for a later return of the sun, in November.

The Mexican agricultural year began in February, at the time when the last rains of the year were coming to an end, and the first signs of the dryer period of spring were apparent. This period was associated with the eastern direction of the sky. The sky itself was, like the earth, thought to have four directions but they were constantly changing in relationship to the earth since the sky was turning around on its polar axis. Thus, the four directions of the sky coincided with the four great seasonal farming festivals, common to all agricultural tribes which lived in the Northern Hemisphere.

The after-life

One implication of Mexican cosmology was the existence of some kind of underworld. Where else could the sun go when it was in the north? The underworld, it seems, had more than one level; for instance, there was a force just a little way below the surface which made growing plants push their way upwards, and burst into flower. Important among the divisions of the underworld was the abode for the majority of dead humans, called Mictlan. Mictlan does not seem to have been a very exciting place to be. At death, providing it was through natural causes, the body was dressed up in fine clothes, a red dog was slaughtered to accompany it on the journey, and often a small package of food was prepared. On the third day the body was cremated, and the soul started its journey with the dog for company.

The road led to the west, and down into the earth. On the way were several terrible ordeals to be faced, such as the clashing rocks—two enormous rocks which leapt together every now and then from the sides of the cave through which the soul wandered. If the soul was caught between them, it was the end: it would be crushed, broken and destroyed. Having negotiated this hazard there was also a narrow mountain ridge, along which the soul had to balance, hoping not to fall on either side. If the soul were successful, however, after three years of the journey, it came to the home of the death gods where life went on happily and there was good company and much feasting and dancing. During the journey, the dead had also been through the wind of knives, where sharp blades of flint had cut all the flesh from their bones. This part of the underworld was, then, populated by living skeletons who held ceremonies and feasts around the court of the great Lord of

Below: Relief in typical style from Tajin, showing the rain god Tlaloc riding on the Earth Monster. This may show a phase of creation which preceded the present earth when the Earth Monster was still beneath the waters

the Dead, Mictlantecuhtli, and his consort, the goddess Mictlantecihuatl.

There is no record of any belief about a further journey of the soul, yet it seems generally to have been thought that, for some at least, there would be a resurrection, and that the souls in the underworld could eventually find their way to the centre, where a living fire continually burned. This central fire suggests that returning souls would take the form of sparks of fire flying upwards, just as sparks flying downwards were souls coming from the creator to take form from a human mother.

This Mexican underworld had several divisions and the land of the dead seems to have included separate states of being. There was a special paradise for babies

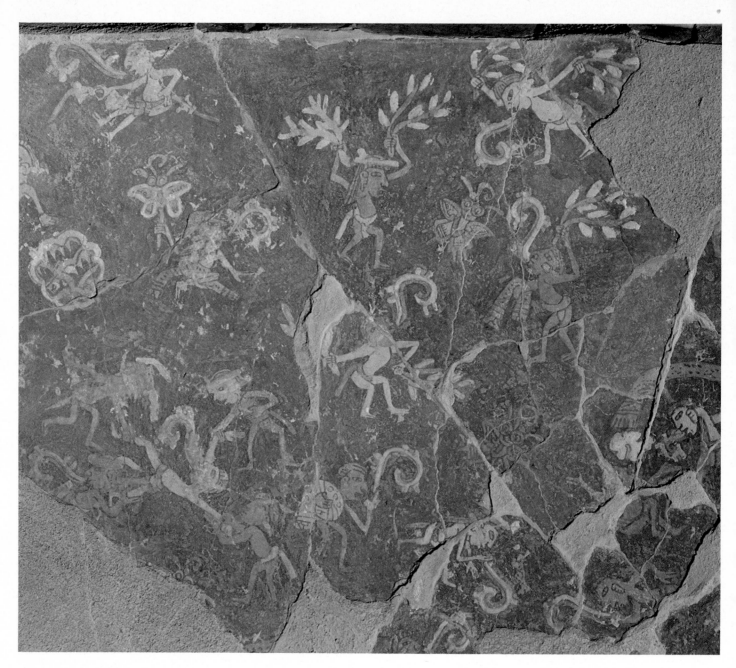

who had died before they were weaned, called the Heaven of the Milk Tree. The small souls went to live in a land where the trees gave fruit in the form of human breasts, which nourished the babies until their time came to be returned to earth.

Another special resting place called Tlalocan was reserved for those who had died by drowning or of diseases associated with water, such as dropsy. It was the home of the rain god and his consort Chalchihuitlicue, the pretty adolescent whose name can be translated as Lady Precious Green. In this heaven the spirits disported themselves, happily playing and constantly singing the praises of the gods in a world which was full of green vegetation, butterflies, and a constant thin rain which reflected rainbows in all directions. To the dwellers on the arid plateau of Mexico, this was a concept of extreme happiness. Thus for those who had died naturally through the waters, there was a place of

Above and above right: Colourful frescoes from Teotihuacan depicting the happy dead who have found a place in Tlalocan, the heaven ruled over by the rain god, Tlaloc. It is shown as a place where, not surprisingly, water abounded. For the people of Mexico, whose lives were at the mercy of drought, this must have been a wonderful prospect. The spirits are shown with scrolls of song coming from their mouths and many of them are dancing with green, leafy boughs in their hands, evidently happy. Butterflies, always an emblem of rich, well-watered vegetation to the Mexicans, abound. On earth they were treated with affection and were thought of as the returning spirits of the dead

Right: Aztec relief showing Tlaloc as lord of Tlalocan, identifiable by his four great teeth. On his chest is the symbol of jade, while attached to his limbs are the skulls of the dead who have entered his paradise

beauty and joy. There was probably some inner connection with fertility rituals in this belief, but it is not explicit in any of the surviving documents.

The highest heaven was a glorious heaven for those who had given their life for the benefit of the nation. A place here was the honourable right of men who had been slain as a result of war, whether it was on the field of battle or in the ritual of sacrifice in the temples. It was equally fitting for all women who had died in childbirth. The men died to defeat the enemies of the country and so to preserve life, the women died in the act of producing life. They were both honoured, and their glory was the glory of the sun, because the sun himself was supposed to be suffering continually. He was constantly calling for blood from the sacrifices in order to assuage his burning thirst.

In this land of glory, eagles accompanied the warriors, carrying messages from the sun to the earth. Both

Above: Totonac pottery figure of the grotesque Lord of the Dead, Mictlantecuhtli. On their way to his sombre under-world the dead were reduced to skeletons by a wind of knives

Right: Wooden mask, inlaid with shell and turquoise, representing Lady Precious Green, Chalchihuitlicue, apparently rising from the jaws of the earth. She is wearing a nose-pendant of a type worn by Aztec women of rank, and her plaited hair is also typical of Aztec fashion

warriors and women were adorned with beautiful garments, wreathed with flowers, and with the most glorious feathers in their hair. They were the honoured, glorious and splendid ones. Whether they continued their tasks in this heaven is not known, but it seems that it was thought of as a final reward. The warriors came rejoicing with the sun as he rose, and led him up to the top of the sky, where the souls of the women took over, brought him down through the western skies, and laid him safely to rest in the underworld before his next daily rising.

The official beliefs about the world of the dead were somewhat confused. A great deal of folklore, as well as practical experience, led the Aztecs and all the subject nations to believe in the appearance of ghosts. In some cases spirits appeared in the natural form of people when they were alive. The function of the ghosts was either to reveal information or to make requests for better behaviour within their families. There were terrifying ghosts of women who had died in child-birth, apparently in violent circumstances, because these were not the companions of the sun, but had come to earth as demonic beings whose appearance presaged death. It was thought that because they were deprived of children they would seek to catch and slay children, or kill any young person who came near them. They were, apparently, beautiful, and the story went that their victims would go to the river to draw some water, and find there, sitting by the bank, a beautiful lady with long, glossy, black hair. As they came near, she would suddenly turn her face and it would be revealed as a bare skull, glaring at them. This was often a fatal vision, for they returned home to fall sick and either be cured through many ceremonies by the priest, or else die.

Diseases were thought of as small, insect-like spirits, that were sent among the people for one reason or another, usually by the gods. They fastened on the victim and sucked away blood, or captured the soul and took it away. However, there were also occasional visits from the happy dead, who came to reassure their relatives that all was well. These souls appeared, most charmingly, as beautiful butterflies which came and flew around the house, and especially around the bou-quets of flowers which were normally carried by Aztec men of any social rank. It was considered ill-mannered to smell a bouquet of flowers from the top: it should always be sniffed at the side, for the top was left for the souls to visit, where they could enjoy the fragrance thus reserved especially for them.

The wheel of time

We should find it quite hard to adjust to the Aztec year. It had no months as we know them, and, indeed, paid no attention to the moon. Instead, each year was

divided into 18 groups of 20 days, which, of course, made up 360. There were five days left over, which people called the 'Nemontemi', or nothing days. On each initial day of a 20-day period there was a great festival in the temples, when people came in their best clothes to take part in the dances and singing. They watched the priests perform sacrifices, often of human beings, but sometimes of animals and fruit, which were made according to the season of the year.

A year of 365 days, however, does not precisely fit the movement of the earth around the sun, and the Aztec priests were aware of the small discrepancy. They made this up in two ways. The first was arranged for the farmers, whose crops must be kept within very close limits to the proper season of the solar year. A leap year was therefore instituted for agricultural purposes, so that every four years an extra day was added, and the ceremonies adjusted accordingly. But for the actual year reckoning, the days were accumulated, and at the end of a period of 52 years, there had to be a correction of 12 days. So, 52 years after the beginning of the calendar round, there was an important festival, lasting over 12 days, which was a time of fasting and penitence. Then, on the midnight of the last day, the priests watched for the overhead passage of the star Aldebaran, known to the Aztecs as the Star of the Fire-Making. As it reached the zenith of the sky, a prisoner was stretched out, his heart removed, and in its place a piece of wood was laid on a plate of turquoise. On this the priest kindled the new fire.

At the beginning of the festival period all fire and all lights were extinguished in the city. When the new fire was kindled, the priests from the temples brought torches which they lit from it. They then took the fire back to light the braziers in their own temples. All the people from the city then came to these temples with torches, in order to rekindle their domestic fires.

Below: Seated figure of Xuihtecuhtli, Lord of Fire, who represented the great creator Ometecuhtli and was present in the hearth of every home. The circles on the head-dress symbolize fire and the top of the head is hollowed out so that fire can be kindled there

Bottom: Every 52 years an Aztec fire-festival called the 'Tying-up of Years' was held. This festival was of great calendrical significance: it brought one bundle of years to a close, and might also bring with it the end of the world. This stone carving represents a bundle of 52 sticks which were to be symbolically burnt during the festival, with the symbol of the year of the festival draped over it

At the end of 104 years, when two of these cycles had been completed, the fire-festival, which was called 'The Tying-up of Years', was extended by another day. Thus the ceremonial calendar was kept in line with true solar time with great accuracy.

Accuracy was important to the priests, and it is clear that they must have spent a great deal of time studying the skies in order to reach such precise knowledge. They were also aware of the saros, the period in which solar eclipses recur after a little more than 19 years. In this period there may be several eclipses, but they always follow a similar pattern through the period of the saros. Of course, most eclipses were only partial ones, but the occasional total eclipse caused great upheavals, since people were afraid that the sun was being captured and destroyed by some terrible monster. Offerings were made. In particular, cripples, especially hunchbacks, were taken from their homes and sacrificed as quickly as possible, so that their spirits would be sent to aid the armies of the sun. As this always succeeded, cripples and hunchbacks were treated very kindly in normal life.

Gods of the heavens

The movement of the planets was also noted down by the astronomer-priests, and formed an important part of their studies, but, except for the planet Venus, they did not greatly affect the life of the common people. Venus was called Tlauixcalpantecuhtli, which means 'Lord of the House of Dawn'. The planet had two aspects, shown as twin gods. One, as Morning Star, was gracious and kindly, and this was the Precious Twin, Quetzalcoatl. He lifted the sun into the sky in the morning. Also he was the god of the wind, of the breath of life, and the protector of all growing things. His darksome twin was Xolotl, a monster with the head of a strange, blunt-faced animal, with long tusks. His feet were twisted, and very often the feet were represented as turned backwards. He was a crooked hunchback, usually shown with a slavering mouth, and at least one eye was always pendant on his cheek instead of being set in the socket. This dreadful monster brought misfortune and trouble, but he was frequently represented because he was the planet Venus as the Evening Star. He was the one who pushed the sun into the darkness and trampled on him, to secure his own elevation. Neither of these gods was considered perfect, because each reached a certain height in the sky, and then declined again towards the horizon, so although day by day each 'star' might appear to be higher and higher, it never reached the top of the sky—the zenith. Instead, day by day, it started to decline until it disappeared. On two periods in the Venus cycle the planet was invisible, a short period of eight days, and a longer period of 180 days. At these times it was thought that

Above: Quetzalcoatl bursts from the serpent's jaws of the earth in his form as Morning Star. Below his head the flaming disc represents the planet itself which is also symbolized by the god's head-dress. Below the disc are two circles with animal heads denoting the date. This stele is pre-Toltec and comes from Santa Lucia Cozumahualpa. Held up towards the god are a sacrificial heart and the head of the victim, which seems to indicate that human sacrifice to Quetzalcoatl was not as rare in pre-Toltec times as it later became, though it is likely that the victims were always noblemen and not mere prisoners

35

Quetzalcoatl was in the underworld, and that the two gods were engaged in some sort of struggle.

The only human sacrifice ever made to Quetzalcoatl was in his periods of invisibility, when nobles of ancient Toltec descent chose one of their numbers to be taken secretly through the carved serpent jaws of the round temple of Quetzalcoatl and slain. At no other period was any human sacrifice made to him, and no person of lesser quality than one of the highest degree of nobles might be sacrificed, since in his lifetime Quetzalcoatl had been the first ruler of the ancient Toltec empire.

As far as the common people were concerned, it was dangerous to go out in the evenings when the Evening Star was shining, for fear that his rays would send darts of illness or even death towards them. But to be shone on by Venus as Morning Star was a matter of great good fortune. It was the custom to cut one's ears with a cactus spine and take two drops of blood on two fingers which were then lifted up to cast the blood in the direction of the Morning Star. This was a little offering of discomfort and life's substance, meant to please the god Quetzalcoatl.

The other visible planets were all well known, and it is possible that there were special ceremonies for them, though nothing is really clear. The planet Mercury was Piltzintecuhtli, a young god (his name means Prince, or Princely Lord) whose hair was golden like the sun. He was symbolically represented by youths who climbed poles to win prizes at the great festivals held for the boys trained in the temple schools.

The Moon, although not directly involved in the calendar, was obviously of considerable interest to the ancient Mexicans. They thought of her in two distinct ways. The most important of these was as the Lady Golden Bells, Coyolxauhqui. She was the sister of the great solar deity, Huitzilopochtli. When Huitzilopochtli was born he leapt forth from the Mother Earth and prepared to slay all the creatures around him. While still in the womb he had heard that the stars and the planets had plotted to destroy him, and he had prepared for revenge. The first being he met he decapitated with a single stroke, and then suddenly realized that it must be his sister, whom he had heard pleading for him. In a moment of penitence he picked up the head and threw it into the sky. There Golden Bells shone, even when all the other stars had gone. When the sun rose in the morning, she could still sometimes be seen in the blue sunlit sky. In the evening, the full beauty of the golden moon could be seen shining among the stars, subduing them with her brilliance, as she passed across the sky.

The other, more magical aspect of the moon was as the goddess Tlazolteotl, the Eater of Filth. This goddess had four phases, and her name arose because in her third phase she would absorb the evils perpetrated by mankind, and purify the soul, if the sinner had made a

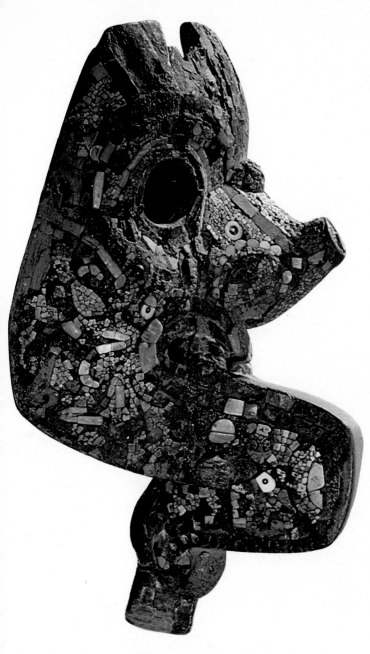

proper and honest confession to her priest. However, confession could only be made once, so it was usually delayed until, at the end of the age of sexual activity, the penitent felt that temptation was no longer a danger. In the first of her four phases, she was the young moon, a brilliant adolescent who was totally unreliable, cruel and yet delightful. For the second phase she changed and became a sensual young woman eager for adventure, a patroness of gambling with a very doubtful morality. The third aspect of the goddess, as the priestess, not only forgave sins as has been described, but also gave blessings to married life and brought peace and fertility to the home. This third aspect, however, was comparatively short-lived; the goddess turned into a Hecate-like monster during her fourth phase, destroying her lovers, stealing wealth, and giving no reward.

Thus, this goddess seems to have been a symbol of the changeability of women. Nevertheless, in all her aspects, she was dressed in moon symbols, and was identified with the moon even though, perhaps, she really may have represented a Freudian fear of femininity among the men of this male-dominated society. Maybe, somewhere at the back of their minds, they held a fear that their sisters and their wives would extract a terrible revenge for their comparative subservience.

In examining the astronomical aspects of ancient Mexican religion, it should be noted that these gods also cover calendrical aspects and thus link with the deities of the earth. In fact, if one plots the sequence of the 18 festivals of the Mexican year, one can see that there is a regular alternation, with a deity of the surface of the earth followed by a sky deity, then back to the surface of the world, and then an underworld deity. The sequence weaves its way through time until the whole series is complete. It is, in fact, slightly more complex than this, and it must be assumed that the whole careful arrangement was originated in the distant past by an astrologer with the mind of a computer. The rhythms are so precise, and the system so carefully planned, that one can do nothing but accept it with admiration. Of course, it is concerned with a flat earth, and, therefore, cannot really be scientifically accurate, but this combination of wheels of time was very practical to the American Indian mind, and easy to understand. They had no wheels for transport, so what they were thinking about was not really a wheel, but the constant rotation of the sky, the spinning of time, and the interrelation of all lesser time rhythms in one great rhythm which was fully completed once every 52 years, when the new fire festival fell due.

Top left and above: Xolotl, the sinister twin of Quetzalcoatl, was the planet Venus as Evening Star and was always represented as a horrifyingly distorted creature. The Aztec pottery figure, top left, shows him with the symbols of the planet on his forehead and covering his eyes. He is destructive, and carries an axe in his right hand. The mask, above, represents him in an even more horribly ugly and evil form, with a drooling mouth and misshapen nose

Left: Teotihuacano carving of the symbol of Tlaloc, the rain god: his four teeth hang above a symbol of growing vegetation

Gods of the earth and air

In the region of the middle air, the rain god, Tlaloc, had his abode. He was Lord of all Sources of Water, and his wife was the young fertility goddess, Lady

Precious Green. At his temple there were four lesser forms of the rain spirit. These were the Tlaloques, and they represented rain clouds of the four directions of the universe. If the offerings were properly made, the great Tlaloc, from his home in the mountains where the cloud mingled with the rocks and the snows, sent forth streams of water to fertilize the earth.

The god would always listen and dispatch an appropriate messenger. Sometimes, the terrible northern rains would come, sweeping down with the wind, now known to modern Mexicans as the *Norte,* bringing hail and thunder. In Aztec symbols, this was a destructive rain, bringing white snow and hail, like the bones of the dead. But if happiness reigned in the rain god's heaven then the eastern rain might be sent. It was thought of as the golden rain which sprinkled lightly over the fields, causing the young plants to sprout their green shoots above the earth, with a promise of life to come. The southern rain was a rich rain of summer fertility, and was thought of as the blue rain, since blue was the sacred colour of Tlaloc himself. The southern rain brought warmth, richness, and growth.

The western rain was a red rain, not of blood, but coloured from the clouds of sunset. It heralded the period of fruitfulness in the autumn. It was the rain of richness and success, before the fields were left fallow for the new planting. Thus, the circuit of the heavens was also the circuit of the seasons, as well as the means of describing different kinds of weather.

The gods of the surface of the earth were somewhat different. Some of them were the spirits of war, with whom we shall deal more fully later, but they also included the vegetation deities. Of these, the most important was the maize spirit, Cinteotl. It is uncertain whether Cinteotl is a god or goddess in this context— at least, until the very end of the sequence of festivals. At the beginning of the secular year in February, the young maize was planted in the earth, and dances to Mother Earth were performed. However, nothing very important in the sequence was observed until, as the warm sun brought forth the fruit on the growing maize canes, there was a great festival of youth, akin to a maypole festival.

As in all the rest of the world, this festival of the first appearance of ears on the corn, and of the young flowers and fruit, was a matter for celebration and happiness. The custom in Mexico was for the girls and young women, even young married women, to undo their hair in loose tresses, like small girls, strip off their ponchoes, and dance bare-breasted to the maize fields. In the fields, each one plucked five ears of green corn and brought them back, dancing and singing in a grand procession. People cast flower petals over them, and bags of scented powder were thrown. Everyone was trying to drench everyone else in scented maize flour or pollen from the flowers. It was a happy occasion, and the breasts of the young girls were the promises of food and life. The young maize plant was symbolized as a pretty goddess, Xilonen, Princess of the Unripe Maize, who is usually shown seated demurely, bare-breasted, and carrying fresh maize cobs in her hands.

As the year progressed the corn ripened, and although in ancient times the cobs were not as monstrous as the modern, chemically cultivated varieties, they were really the staff of life for Mexico. The newly reaped maize cobs were brought home to the cribs, but the last five cobs were packed up very carefully by the old women. These were carried in baskets on their backs, wrapped in cloth, as if they were babies. They were made much of, were looked after well, and sacrifices were offered in front of them. Then they were put in a special basket in the corn crib, outside the house, because they were the symbol of the maize spirit. Here was life in abeyance, life which was resting, before it came forth in the next year.

The five cobs were symbols of another very much worshipped goddess, the Lady Chicomecoatl, Seven Serpents. She was the earth spirit, lady of fertility, lady of life, who was responsible for caring for life as a kind of great mother of the people.

There were other important goddesses in Mexico connected with fertility. One is represented by the enormous statue, now in the National Museum in Mexico City, which is known as Coatlicue, the Mother Earth. She is one of a pair who stood in the courtyard of the great temple. When the building was destroyed, one of these statues was toppled over, broken into pieces, and much of it has been lost. The other one, apparently, just fell over and was covered with rubble and burning timbers during that terrible last battle. She lay covered up, and was eventually covered with earth which has since formed the basis for the Zocalo, the square in front of the modern cathedral. It was there

that William Bullock, an English traveller, saw the site excavated in 1824. Every year since the conquest of Mexico, people had come during an autumn festival with gifts of fruit and flowers which they laid on the pavement of the central square. It was all very innocent, and was, in fact, accepted as something pious in the Christian sense. The Indians always maintained that there was somebody very holy and powerful underneath. The excavation revealed the enormous statue of Mother Earth.

Mother Earth was without property, though she was much worshipped. The world was made from her body, she owned nothing, and her garment is made from rattlesnakes, for the earth was believed to shelter the rattlesnake in holes in the ground. The rattlesnake was a symbol of poverty because of its habit of living in these holes, so Mother Earth was always girdled with poverty. Her feet were enormous claws, symbolizing

the digging of graves into the earth. Her hands, too, were claw-like. Her head was made up of two facing heads of enormous rattlesnakes, the pattern on their skin showing that they represented turquoise, the precious fire-jewel. Around her neck she wears a garland, and the neck itself is shown as the top of a 'Cuauhxicalli', an eagle vase, which was used for holding the hearts of human sacrifices. This is accompanied by a necklace made of hands and hearts. The palm of the hand of a human sacrifice was supposed to be so wonderful to eat that it was reserved for the pleasure of rulers and great noblemen who were present at the ceremonies. The hearts were the hearts of sacrifice, and they represented the pain that Mother Earth must have had in giving birth to all her children. It was the pain that man suffers throughout his life in hard work and the struggle for existence.

The whole monstrous sculpture of Coatlicue is

Left: Turquoise encrusted Aztec mask of the sun god, Tonatiuh. The eyes and teeth are made of shell and the turquoise represents fire. Life-size masks such as this one were tied onto the images of the gods in Tenochtitlan

Below: The youthful figure of Lady Precious Green, Chalchihuitlicue, who was a fertility goddess and consort to Tlaloc. Her youth is indicated by the style of her hair, while her status as a goddess is shown by the head-dress fringed with aramanth seeds and by the tassels adorning her cape which symbolize flowers. She is squatting on her heels in a manner typical of Mexican women

Left: The goddess Coyolxauhqui, Lady Golden Bells, was the most important aspect of the moon. On this enormous Aztec monolithic head, the bells are shown hanging from her cheeks. She wears a moon-shaped nose-pendant and the lower parts of the ornaments hanging from her ears are symbols indicating the lunar role in the regulation of time

almost terrifying to a European, but, in reality, it is a poem to Mother Earth to thank her for her pain and kindness in giving food and life to mankind. At death, man is returned to Mother Earth, and this is symbolized by the human skull over her heart. This great sculpture expresses in its own mighty way the relationship between the Aztec people of the glorious city of Tenochtitlan and the earth.

The other goddess of the earth was the lady of the earth's surface, and apparently of some little way below, because she was a guardian of graves. Primarily she was the goddess of flowers, of happiness, and of love-making, which even in Aztec Mexico could mean romantic love. Her name was Xochiquetzal. She was thought of as an extremely beautiful lady, in fact her name means beautiful flowers: 'xochitl' meant flower, and 'quetzal' meant precious or beautiful—it was also the name of the quetzal bird, whose beautiful green

feathers adorned the head-dresses of the gods and rulers. Xochiquetzal is usually shown with flowers in her head-dress, as a young married woman wearing a wrap-around skirt and a Quechquimitl, or embroidered poncho.

Xochiquetzal's particular flower was the marigold. In modern Mexico, many towns and villages celebrate the day of the dead, or All Souls, at the beginning of November, with a night meal to which the souls of departed members of the family are invited to come. They are told the news of the family and the hopes that the parents hold for the next generation, and they are asked to pray for them in the heaven to which they will return the following morning. Meanwhile, the ground is strewn with marigolds, which, even nowadays, are the flowers for the day of the dead. Thus, an ancient ritual has become a touching and pleasant modern custom.

Quetzalcoatl: the Feathered Serpent

Above: The major symbol of the god Quetzalcoatl is the Feathered Serpent, a serpent wearing the beautiful feathers of the quetzal bird. In this relief from Tenochtitlan the serpent is shown descending between two symbols of years, differentiated from those of days by the boxes carved around them. This carving might represent many different things, one possible interpretation being the Morning Star descending in the sky until it coincides with the rising sun. The dates cover a period of 20 years, and the one on the left is Ce Acatl, which was the year of the rebuilding of the great temple in Tenochtitlan

Left: This green jade figure of Quetzalcoatl shows the god wearing a collar symbolic of the sun. This possibly commemorates a transit of Venus in 1508. In his right hand the god is holding a studded club, while in his left is a skull, the emblem of his terrifying twin deity, Xolotl. This figure, now in the British Museum, is among the most beautiful of many which show the god in this aspect, rising from the jaws of the Feathered Serpent, just as the Morning Star rises from the earth to herald the sunrise. For this reason his ear-rings have pendant ocelot claws, since the roaring of this creature was also believed to bring the sun into the sky ·

Quetzalcoatl, the Feathered Serpent, Lord of Healing and magical herbs, the symbol of learning, 'of poetry and of all things beautiful, the Lord of Hope and the brilliant Lord of the Morning Star, was the spirit who brought up the sun in the morning and thus brought the beneficent power of the sun god to all humans, animals and vegetation. One of the most important figures in the religion of pre-Columbian Mexico, Quetzalcoatl was, rather like the English King Arthur, both a real person and a myth. The King Quetzalcoatl was the founder of an empire, and of a way of life which differed from that of other Mexican societies mainly by being more deeply religious. His greatest success was to form a confederation of tribal groups under the domination of the Toltec families, who supported a sequence of divine kings, each one of whom was called the Quetzalcoatl, though they also had their own personal names.

The story of the first great king Quetzalcoatl relates how he came from heaven to earth and founded a dominion among the people of Mexico where he lived as a celibate, holy priest, until a dispute among the gods led to his destruction. While at a great ceremony, Quetzalcoatl was plied with strong drink laced with the magic mushroom. Tempted by the demonic goddess who inhabited the mushrooms, he seized her and copulated during the feast. On awakening from his poisoned sleep he realized that he had condemned himself. Giving up all his palaces, he travelled across Mexico until he arrived naked on the shores of the Caribbean Sea. There he embarked on a raft of serpent skins, and sailed far away, towards the sunrise, until the tremendous heat ignited the boat and his heart arose, flying up to join the sun.

There is a picture of the glorious event in the Vienna Codex which represents a real solar eclipse, in which the planet Venus was seen close to the sun. As this is an extremely rare occurrence, the Royal Observatory at

Greenwich could date the occasion precisely: July 16, AD 750—an accurate historical date for the death of a divine king, who has entered the realms of mythology. According to the Vienna Codex a series of nine Toltec kings, each of whom was called Quetzalcoatl, followed the first great ruler. Each is depicted making fire on his accession and is credited with the erection of temples and sweat baths. Each royal succession is very carefully recorded, so that it has been possible to date the whole line of Toltec kings, ending with the fall of Tula under the last Quetzalcoatl, in the final decade of the tenth century.

In the stories of his adventures on earth, Quetzalcoatl is shown as a sexually potent being, whose energies were pent up until he was tempted by the goddess Tlazoteotl. In all descriptions of his personality, he is said to have been active and vigorous, and to have had an enormous penis. He wore a special loin-cloth with a rounded end, apparently as a bag in which to stow this marvellous organ. In a painting in the *Codex Laud* in the Bodleian Library, Oxford, he is seen as a wind blowing in the waters; sitting within the water, displaying her open vulva to him, is the younger moon goddess. The implication is that the breath of Quetzalcoatl is the fertilizing breath of life, and that the goddess will be impregnated by it.

The god Quetzalcoatl was also the Lord of Life, who brought penitence, love, and exemption from the usual rituals of sacrifice and blood offering, and he was, therefore, a figure of divine wisdom and love. Thus he could be understood, even by the early missionaries from Spain, as a being not wholly demonic, even though he was often shown under the strange guise of a serpent clothed in the green feathers of the quetzal bird.

Aspects of the Feathered Serpent

The Feathered Serpent is one of the great mysteries of ancient Mexican belief. In ancient times the quetzal, a native of the western mountains of Guatemala, also lived in Mexico. It was regarded as the most beautiful of all birds and its name, Quetzaltotolin, means the most precious, or the most beautiful bird. The symbol of the feathered serpent can well be called Quetzalcoatl, which means not just the 'feathered serpent', but the 'most precious serpent', though, to be iconographically correct the god Quetzalcoatl is not himself the feathered serpent, but the one who emerges from the serpent, just as the Morning Star rises from the horizon. The most beautiful images of the god illustrate this aspect: a limestone example in the National Museum in Mexico City shows the face of the god in the serpent's mouth, as he retires at sunset, and there is a remarkable jade statue in the British Museum in which the god is shown arising from the serpent like the sun rising at dawn.

The Aztec language often had words of the same sound, but with different meanings. The word 'coatl' not only means serpent, it also means a twin; in this case, the twins are the Morning Star and the Evening Star, Quetzalcoatl and Xolotl. The god referred to as the Feathered Serpent, should thus really be described as the Precious Twin, since 'quetzal' means both 'the bird' and 'precious'. A great confusion could have been avoided if more attention had been paid in the past to the meaning of the words, rather than to the appearance of the symbol, which was merely a literal representation.

Other representations indicate different aspects of the god. Occasionally, statues show him as a very great priest, the Lord of Penitence, his face painted with black strips beside the eyes, a red ring around the mouth, and large areas of blue on the forehead. As Quetzalcoatl

Above: In this stele Quetzalcoatl as Morning Star is shown emerging from the jaws of a serpent—its forked tongue can be seen lolling from its lower jaw. The stele is proto-Toltec in style and is from Azcapotzalco, a city founded by refugees after the fall of Teotihuacan

Left: This shell head may have been removed from Quetzalcoatl's palace of shell in Tollan, and shows the god rising from the jaws of earth. The heavy black beard would be peculiar among American Indians

45

Ehecatl, Lord of the Winds, he is shown wearing a mask that projects like a pointed snout covering the lower part of his face. This is known as the 'wind mask', and is usually painted a bright red. It was probably derived from the snout of the Mexican whistling toad, *Rhinophryne dorsalis,* and, by its shape, suggested to the Mexican mind the shape of the Earth Monster, a cross between an alligator and a toad. A temple dedicated to Ehecatl was circular in plan, for as a god of the wind he could blow or breathe in any direction and therefore could not be confined to a square structure facing only the four cardinal points. In the Vienna Codex, Quetzalcoatl, as the wind god, is shown supporting the heaven with his hands. The heaven is the heaven of waters, and, in effect, he is holding the rain clouds above the earth, and showering out their waters as they are driven from place to place before the wind. As god of the weather, the wind and the rain, Quetzalcoatl joins the hierarchy of the vegetation gods. His function as the wind is to dry the soil, and to prepare the earth for the coming of the rains.

At other times he is just a god of springtime and rising vegetation, similar to the western Asian vegetation gods, who suffered, and who were either driven away or killed. Quetzalcoatl, as a ruler on earth, also had to leave his wealth, his garments, and finally his life, before he could be taken into the heavens and made into the Morning Star. It is as this self-sacrificing god who became the Morning Star that he is the god of springtime and of rising life.

The position of this god is an important measure of social development in Mexican history. Firstly, he was a god of springtime, and the beneficent winds. Secondly, he was an astrological deity of the Morning Star. Thirdly, he came to be regarded as the founder of kingship. At each stage the god symbolized a further advance in civilization. In his final position as the king who was and is to be, Quetzalcoatl had become the

46

highest expression of divine kingship that had yet been evolved in Central America. The Uetlatoani, or Great Speaker, of the Aztec tribe was so entitled because he spoke as a ruler of many subject tribes. The idea of the imperialist overlord ruling a predatory military state was a true reflection of the condition of Mexican civilization when Hernando Cortes arrived in 1519.

The origins of Quetzalcoatl

The historical origins of Quetzalcoatl and his cult are as complex as his position in the hierarchy of Mexican gods. Although it is possible to date the Toltecs' god in *Codex Vindobonensis* and to trace his descendants as kings, it seems probable that the cult of Quetzalcoatl had more ancient origins still. Whether or not Toltec culture, the inspiration of the Aztecs, was drawn entirely from an earlier time we do not know. It is likely that the rulers of the great ruined city of Teotihuacan, which flourished from the first century BC until about AD 650, were a more primitive type of divine kings or priest-kings. Another possibility is that the Toltecs included a group from the Pacific coast of Mexico, who had brought with them the Toltec style calendar and the cult of Quetzalcoatl.

It is not possible to identify with certainty any figures which could represent Quetzalcoatl in the art of Teotihuacan, but to the south of the Aztec region, among the Maya tribes, there was a true equivalent to the god Quetzalcoatl, who was called Kukulcan. This name means quetzal bird-serpent, the exact equivalent of Quetzalcoatl. The Maya god was also the god of the wind and giver of jewels; he protected growing things, and to some extent he was a fertility god. There are few recognizable images until later times, but when the Maya had fallen under domination by Toltec refugees from the fall of Tula, we find Kukulcan, with his name written in Maya syllabic characters, painted on a cap-stone from Chichen Itzá, in Yucatan. Here he is shown in the centre of a sun symbol; the picture almost certainly represents a transit of Venus in the twelfth century AD. The Maya god is wearing a wind mask with an extended snout, similar to that shown on Aztec figures, and is disposing of jewels and showering blessings on the earth.

An earlier form of Kukulcan among the Maya is associated with the Moan bird, which appears on a foliated cross in Palenque in southern Mexico. This bird has the plumage of a quetzal with a serpent-like head rather like the wind mask. It is shown also on a stele from El Castillo, on the western coast of Guatemala, flying across the face of the sun. As there are other astronomical data, it is conclusively shown to have been a representation of a transit of Venus which took place in the sixth century AD, two centuries before the Toltecs had entered Mexico. This group of examples

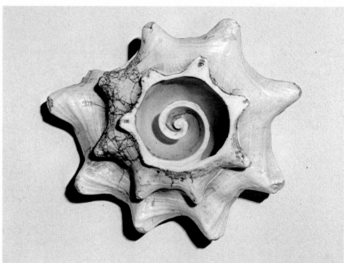

Above: Among the many aspects of Quetzalcoatl was that of the Lord of the Winds, Ehecatl. Temples dedicated to him in this aspect were circular in shape because, as the wind, he was not restricted to any one direction. Thus this clay model of a temple from northern Mexico, with its circular god-houses, probably represents a temple dedicated to Quetzalcoatl as Ehecatl. Model temples like this were fairly common objects, possibly used as shrines in the home. Below it is the symbol of the god as Lord of the Winds, a conch shell cut in a cross-section and often called the 'wind jewel'. This was probably worn by priests

shows clearly that the idea of the god Quetzalcoatl as the breath of life, the most precious symbol of life and of wind, pre-dates the introduction of Toltec religion into highland Mexico.

Quetzalcoatl and the Aztecs

For the Aztecs the most important aspect of the cult of Quetzalcoatl was his position as ancestor of the Toltec kings because it was this which conferred the divine right to rule. The Aztec chiefs went to great lengths to justify their own divine right, partly by altering their original records, but mostly by carefully marrying princesses of Toltec descent into their ruling families. Just as the Toltec Empire, ruled in turn by the nine Quetzalcoatls, had absorbed all the civilized regions of Mexico, so the Aztecs hoped that through the divine right, which came by descent from Quetzalcoatl, they would also rule over an expanding empire. This was quite different from their military cults of the mighty war god, the Smoking Mirror, Tezcatlipoca, for it was a matter of right, rather than might. Yet because they could not successfully prosecute wars without the blessing of Tezcatlipoca, the Lord of the Surface of the Earth, and had no right to fight without the true traditional descent from the first Quetzalcoatl, the two cults were inextricably interwoven.

Although Quetzalcoatl was still of tremendous import to the leaders of the nation, it is clear that at the time when the Spaniards came, the younger people, even of the more important families, had not been initiated into the cult of the god. It seems, too, that it had become a cult peculiar to the nobles, which was not talked about among the common people who were unaware of the secret sacrifice of one of the nobility of Toltec descent when the Morning Star was invisible.

In the accounts of ceremonies in the Aztec calendar not one of the 20-day periods was dedicated to Quetzalcoatl. He was only mentioned in the first month Atlcaualo, as Lord of the Winds, who made clear the path of the rain gods. None of the 20-day periods has any reference to him, but every time the day Ce Acatl, which means one, arrow-reed and was the name given to the Morning Star, came round, they made special offerings and danced in honour of Quetzalcoatl.

As in Toltec times, Quetzalcoatl was still the master of all works of art from the hardest jade to the softest feathers and all the advanced craftsmen were dependent on the artist-priests who served the god. It was these skilled servants of Quetzalcoatl who alone decorated and painted the great temples and palaces of Aztec Mexico with pictures of the gods. Very little of this work remains, partly through deliberate destruction by the Spanish conquerors in the sixteenth century, and partly through slow decomposition through the ages, which turned the plaster into crumbling powder.

Above: As Lord of the Winds, Quetzalcoatl became a god associated with vegetation and fertility. Here he is shown as a bearer of grain, in the form of an Aztec tameme, or porter. His load consists of five maize cobs, the symbol of the maize goddess, and is carried on his back in typical Aztec fashion, using a strap which passes over the forehead. This figure was once covered with stucco and painted

Archaeologists using modern chemical sprays have succeeded in preserving some of these works, but they are lamentably few in number. These artists were also responsible for the designs on wooden objects, on sculptures with which temples and palaces were adorned, and on the few small golden objects which have survived from ancient times. No doubt there was also much silver, but most of it found in recent excavations had already turned into black heaps of silver oxide.

The sculptures of the temples were mostly made from local rock, though harder rocks were sometimes brought in from outlying districts. Hard forms of lava were often used, including basalt, but most of the carving was done on a soft porous rock, like a coarse and rather rough pumice stone, which was called Tezontli. This rock had a most unfortunate pitted surface when carved, so most of the sculptures were covered in cement, carefully polished and then painted. Only one or two examples of this work survive in complete form, which are now in the National Museum in Mexico City.

Originally, all the statues were painted as brilliantly and as fully with symbolic decoration as in the codices. Even the so-called great calendar stone which stood halfway up the staircase of the great temple in Mexico City was brilliantly painted. The painting on this stone has been fully reconstructed through micrographic analysis of powder found in the pores of the stone, so that it has been possible to draw out coloured reproductions, which are brilliant and vivid, although they might appear almost barbarous to our eyes. Sometimes smaller figures preserve slight traces of paint, but there are very few that show the full complexity of design.

During the period of his work the sculptor was considered sacred. He had to leave his family, and live in a special enclosure in the temple courtyard, where he worked with his stone chisels and wooden maul. Only when his work was finished was he released from his diet of three or four dried *tortillas* and a few cups of water per day. His work was then taken to the priests' quarters to be painted, and he himself was loaded with gifts, mantles, feather ornaments and fine food, which he took home to his family. He enjoyed not only the glory of being an artist, but the joy of being reunited with wife and children, and being allowed to eat whatever food could be prepared in his household.

We do not know whether there were similar restrictions on the work of wood-carvers. Although the Aztecs had bronze it was a very uncertain material. A sharp cut is better made from a shark's tooth, a flake of obsidian, a polished down piece of porphyry, or even jade. The few wood-carvings that remain are excellently worked and every line is carved with the sense of the total rhythm of the whole object. An excellent example is the Huehuetl, or standing drum, on which the sun is glorified as the eagle rising from the waters of war.

Opposite page: Two views of the upper section of a Totonac stele. The front, on the left, shows Quetzalcoatl wearing his traditional cone-shaped hat, a necklace, ear-rings and, on his chest, the wind jewel. There is also a jewel thrust through his nose, showing Toltec influence. On the back of the stele, at the bottom of the part shown, is the symbol of a sacrificial heart, while at the top is the fierce head of the Earth Monster, who, according to some legends, was the mother of Quetzalcoatl

Below: In Aztec times, small pottery idols were kept in the home. This fragment shows the head of Quetzalcoatl as Ehecatl, readily identified by the mask projecting like a snout from his mouth, known as the 'wind mask'

In all matters of life and beauty, the god Quetzalcoatl was thought to have breathed and brought life and inspiration. It was in the world of creative achievements that he was supreme. Here, the terrible dark instinctive power from the unconscious, which was Tezcatlipoca, could have no final victory.

The more popular Aztec function of Quetzalcoatl seems to have been as Lord of the Winds, and the one who carried the waters of the sky above his head, though it was customary to offer two drops of blood from the ear when one saw the Morning Star. This accords well enough with the evidence derived from archaeological findings in Mexico City, in which the sculptures of the god almost invariably show him wearing the wind-mask, and only the beautiful jade in the British Museum shows him as the Lord of the Morning Star, rising from the Feathered Serpent.

There was another aspect of Quetzalcoatl, as a spirit of healing, and it is possible that this came from the good fortune associated with Morning Star. It may also have been derived from the thought of the wayward-ness of the wind which might determine matters of health or sickness. The clearest account of this aspect appears in the post-conquest document, *Codex Maglia-becciano*, which is preserved in the National Library of Florence. On page 78 of this Codex there is an account written in about 1550, in Spanish, facing a pictorial representation. It records how when a person fell ill, a healer, often female, was brought in. She placed the patient in front of her, and behind her she placed an image of the god Quetzalcoatl. Then she listened to the descriptions of the infirmity, and proceeded to cast a divination. Between herself and the patient she laid a piece of clean cloth. She then took a shell and placed a handful of grains of maize, both light and dark in colour, in it and threw them out onto the cloth. If one grain fell upon another it was a sign of a rapid recovery. If they fell evenly spaced, recovery would take place gently and steadily without any trouble. The terrible omen, which both parties feared, was when the maize grains fell on the cloth in two separate groups with a clear pathway between them; this would mean that the patient would be separated from life in this world, and the illness would certainly be fatal. In this instance, Quetzalcoatl was a god of fortune, and the breath of life, but there is nothing in the description or in the picture to suggest that he determined the way in which the maize grains would fall. But it is an important illustration of how, among ordinary people of the Aztec community, the god Quetzalcoatl retained some of his high prestige.

It had long been known that just as Quetzalcoatl had been overthrown in the past, so in the coming time he would return and overthrow his adversaries, and bring a reign of greater peace and justice. This almost messianic hope was to be realized in a sad and cruel way when the Spaniards arrived in Mexico and proceeded to overthrow the Aztec empire. The new Quetzalcoatl appeared as a most ruthless warrior, who not only opposed the god of the Aztecs themselves, but caused the overthrow of all other rival deities through-out Mexico. The *débâcle* was complete and terrifying.

Among the common people, once the terrors of the conquest and the accompanying plagues were over, the teachings of the missionaries were accepted. Those black-robed priests, who wore garments very similar to those which had clothed the ancient god, were the messengers of Christian peace, and their god had offered

himself as the once and only sacrifice for the benefit of all mankind. It seemed to the Mexicans that prophecy was fulfilled, and that the new Quetzalcoatl was a god of peace and justice. They flocked in their tens of thousands to be baptized, to receive the blessing of this new aspect of the Morning Star. Although they had ample reason to distrust the Christians, who had been enjoined to teach them religion, they held to the new faith. In many ways they translated it into their own ways of thought, so that the Easter festivals were thought of as celebrations of the return of the god, and of the sweeping away of old evils. In this manner, the ancient cult of Quetzalcoatl survived as an aspect of Christianity, but the name of the old god and the temple rituals disappeared, along with the images and cults of the many other deities.

In modern Mexico the figure of Quetzalcoatl often replaces the more familiar Santa Claus at New Year

parties or in department store windows. The bearer of gifts wears a plume of feathers, and a mask representing the old god, as the bringer of life, of gifts and of happiness to people. In this he has assumed a place that was not really his in the old days, because he was not a god of the regular calendar at all, nor of the changing of the year. Nevertheless, the idea of the gifts of good things are matters in which both the ancient Aztec religion and Christian imagery could well come together. The cult of the god and the poetry associated with him, however, remain as a province of artists and archaeologists, rather than of the mass of Mexican people. The god appears with tremendous vigour on some of the new frescoes, particularly those by José Clemente Orozco, which represent Quetzalcoatl as a great power, like a wind destroying the old dead past and hopefully bringing in a new era of hope for mankind, and for Mexico in particular.

Above: The desolate ruins of Tollan, the Toltec capital, caught in the last light of day. The atmosphere of this abandoned city held magic for the successors of the Toltecs, the Aztecs. The rulers of the Aztecs, the Great Speakers, were all of Toltec descent and therefore counted Quetzalcoatl among their forebears. The Aztecs held strongly to the traditional prophecy of the Toltecs that the god Quetzalcoatl would return, bringing destruction to Aztec society, based as it was on the worship of Tezcatlipoca, the embodiment of the forces opposed to the Feathered Serpent. The last Great Speaker, Montezuma, often visited this lonely spot, and here he must have contemplated the prophecy which he eventually believed to have been fulfilled with the arrival of Cortes

Tezcatlipoca: the Smoking Mirror

Above: This panel from the Codex Fejervary-Mayer shows how Tezcatlipoca tempted the Earth Monster to come to the surface of the great waters by using his foot as bait. She swallowed up his foot, but in the struggle lost her lower jaw. Hideously crippled, she was unable to sink back into the depths and the earth as we know it was created from her body. The symbols at the base of this drawing represent dates, and, with the twelve dots also in the picture, signify the periods in the calendar when Tezcatlipoca was dominant over other forces

Left: The two warriors shown in this detail from a Toltec pottery vessel wear bird head-dresses, showing them to be nobles of very high rank. The equipment and dress of warriors in ancient Mexico varied very little from society to society, but in Toltec times a back shield was worn to protect the kidneys. Both figures are wearing nose-plugs, signs of distinction reserved for great warriors

Life in ancient Mexico was based to a great extent on the worship of the gods, but the gods were not by any means all good-natured or helpful. The most powerful of the earthly spirits was Tezcatlipoca, whose name means Smoking Mirror. This referred to a mirror, made of the volcanic glass known as obsidian, which seers would gaze at until they fell into a trance. Then, within the black, glossy surface, they saw pictures which revealed the future of the tribe and the will of the gods. The Aztecs believed that scrying was a powerful kind of magic granted to them by this shadowy god. Tezcatlipoca gave them control over the other nations; he promised the Aztec people that they should rule over the whole of Anahuac, from the deserts of the north to the mountains of the south, and from the Pacific Ocean to the Caribbean Sea. This great power accomplished his purpose through the vigour of the Aztec armies and the wise tactical decisions of their Great Speakers.

Tezcatlipoca was a representative of the heavens traversed by the sun. In midsummer, as the high sun in the southern sky, he was the special patron of the Aztecs, under his name of Huitzilopochtli, the 'Blue Hummingbird on the left'. This name may have been derived through staring at the sun, since this produces a spot of blue if the eyes are then closed. It was 'on the left' because when facing in the direction of the sun's path, that is to say from east to west, the sun passed to the left.

In the night sky the symbol of the god Tezcatlipoca could be seen as the group of stars we call the Great Bear. To the Aztecs, this was the single footprint of the god who had lost his other foot when he drew the earth out of the waters in the titanic struggle before mankind was created. The god tempted the Earth Monster to come to the surface of the waters and drew her on with his enormous foot. The gigantic monster snapped off his foot, but he in turn tore off her lower

Right: This extraordinary head shows the god Xipe Totec in the form of a warrior wearing, as a mask, the flayed skin of his sacrificed prisoner. Xipe Totec was one of the aspects of Tezcatlipoca particularly identified with suffering and sacrifice. The back of the head, shown below, bears the major symbol of Tezcatlipoca, the Smoking Mirror. Smoke and a tongue of flame can be seen rising from the circular mirror to which are attached small clumps of sacrificial down. These white, downy eagle feathers were thrown onto cuts on the body of a sacrificial victim. They must have stuck to the blood, and this was intended to help in uniting the victim with the stars and the sky

jaw, and she never again sank back into the waters. On her rugged back all the tribes of men were created and lived.

The god who drew the earth from the waters was not a spirit of goodness, however, and because of his imperfections he could never approach the Pole Star, the symbol of the divine duality. Instead he hopped around the Pole Star on his one foot, forming the circumpolar track of the Great Bear in the sky.

Mankind was simply forced to co-exist with this awesome being. It is unusual to find a nation devoted to the service of a demiurge whom we, in a European tradition, would regard as evil in his innermost nature. The only possible parallel is among some of the early dynastic Egyptian kings, who worshipped Set, the spirit of the desert and its terrors. In psychological terms, Tezcatlipoca represents the equivalent of what might be called the 'shadow'—the side of our human personality that we do not wish to face openly, and which we consequently hide from ourselves.

In spite of the many complexities, and the apparent confusion of Aztec theology, the real position of Tezcatlipoca was as a god ruling the earth's surface. In the east his colour was yellow in honour of the rising sun, and the fruitfulness of the maize plant. The southern Tezcatlipoca was the Blue Hummingbird. In the west his colour was red, and symbolized the blood of sacrifice. In the north was the field of the black Tezcatlipoca, who was the spirit of witchcraft and black magic. In no aspect was the god separated from the concepts of magic and sacrifices. One of his names was Titlauacan, which means 'he who is closest to the shoulder'. He was thought to be present on every shoulder, whispering thoughts into the mind, suggesting violence and trickery. In all his forms he was the patron of warriors and of war—a dangerous and deadly being, who brought great material gain and glory to his servants, the Aztec people.

Tezcatlipoca formed a total contrast to the spirit of Quetzalcoatl. The Smoking Mirror was for ever bound to be an adversary of the Feathered Serpent. This was the basic dualism in Mexican religion. Although the actions of Smoking Mirror were dangerous and violent, the Aztecs would not have called this god 'evil'. In fact, it is hard to find anything in Mexican theology that they would call evil, apart from cowardice or an insult to the gods. The contrast was simply between darkness and light, and darkness was the essence of Tezcatlipoca.

The idea of goodness itself does not seem to be at all important in Mexican belief. The good man or woman was simply one who kept to the ritual observances each day and who did not seek any particular pleasures or happiness for himself. It seems strange to the mind

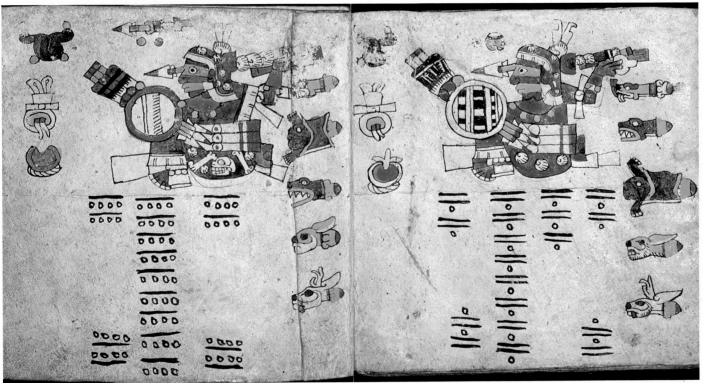

of a European that what we would consider to be evil behaviour was taken by the Mexicans to be the result of the time of one's birth. If a priest, on consulting astrological charts at the birth of a child, found that the future was going to be one of cowardice, theft and adultery, it was still accepted as the will of the gods. So, if the child developed such characteristics in later life, nothing could be done about it, except to make out the pre-ordained punishments for such crimes. This usually meant a death penalty of some particularly unpleasant type. But again this was not particularly the will of the chiefs toward the individual, but simply the working of fate. If doomed to live in such a way, then the individual was simply doomed to die as a natural consequence, and that was that. There was no means of

altering fate. Some hoped that by presenting gifts to the gods, and by building additions to their temples, they could obtain some greater regard and perhaps some minor amelioration of their predicted fate, but it could never alter the main stream of destiny. That was forever unchangeable.

The legend of the destruction of the Toltecs as it filtered through time to the Aztecs, told how Tezcatlipoca turned himself into a great giant who came up against the Toltecs, and caused himself to be killed. The enormous carcass lay on the earth rotting, and so started a pestilence which killed many many thousands of the fated Toltecs. And the story tells, too, how he tempted the daughter of the high chief of the Toltecs when he appeared in the market-place in the form of a naked Huaxtec trader, painted half blue and half red, with a penis so beautiful that she was overcome by desire. Their child was the ill-fated Huemac, who saw the total collapse of Toltec power in Mexico. In all the legends, Tezcatlipoca as the 'shadow' was the cause of the downfall of the Toltecs and their rulers, the Quetzalcoatls. Tezcatlipoca may, too, have been the cause of the change in the calendrical system which occurred at about this time: when the day on which the year began was unaccountably changed. We are also very much in the dark about why, in fact, the adoration of Quetzalcoatl was so important to the Toltecs. They were the most warlike of the Aztec predecessors, and yet gave second place to Tezcatlipoca who was the very incarnation of the spirit of warfare and cruelty.

There appears to have been no chief or king named after either Tezcatlipoca or Huitzilopochtli, and no legend suggests that he was ever a human ruler on earth like Quetzalcoatl. This dark shadow was an entity in itself—a non-material being, a great and terrible spirit who was responsible for bloodshed and for compulsive magic. He was insignificant when compared to the great power, Ometecuhtli, but among the other gods of Mexico he was a giant, and during the Aztec period totally overshadowed all of them.

The cult of the god Tezcatlipoca does not clearly appear until at least late Toltec times, that is approximately the tenth century AD. Whether the idea of a shadow spirit was new or not is unclear. The movement of tribes in earlier times is not known, but when the qualities of the god are considered, he seems more and more a figure from the North American Indians. He is the 'trickster', but less friendly than in the Winnebago or Haida Indian myths. His abilities as a shape-changer and one who leads people into danger are quite clear, and the cult of warriors which was so closely connected with him is very similar to the cult of various warrior societies among the Plains Indians. It is just possible that the cult of Tezcatlipoca, reflecting a deep-seated element of the human psyche, may have been brought into prominence in Mexico through invasions from the north, possibly by the tribes known in later times as the Chichimeca. The name Chichimeca was originally an insult: it meant 'the people who just say Chi Chi Chi when they speak', implying that they could not be understood by civilized people. In time, however, many Chichimec descendants became so important in Mexico that the term became an honourable one and referred to a noble ancestor.

Tezcatlipoca thus became a very powerful god, and the actual comprehension of his nature and power reveals a high level of psychological understanding on the part of the Mexican priests. They had, however, externalized the god, and saw him as something outside themselves, coming to the ceremonies from the other-world of darkness which he inhabited.

The warrior

To the peoples of ancient Mexico there was no question that war was a duty, and that cities must strive to control one another. It was fully accepted that the patron gods of the cities were the victors in the struggle and those that died, died for the honour of their gods. The secret of the continuous series of victories for the Aztecs lay in their assured belief that their god Tezcatlipoca would lead them on to the fulfilment of his promise that they should rule the whole of Anahuac, from the Atlantic to the Pacific. In achieving this, the Aztecs evolved a formidable military organization. Youths were conscripted at the age of 17 or 18 for a period of intensive training which rarely lasted more than five years. Most boys, from an early age, were encouraged to play with toy shields and spears, and gangs of them got together and imitated the battle tactics of the grown-ups. Later on they went through a phase of education which included a great deal of combat training. It was important that they should grow up inured to the hardship of blows and cuts received in fighting, so that they would not weaken when the actual strain of combat fell upon them.

The normal equipment of a Mexican warrior was his ordinary clothing—a loin-cloth and a cloak in which he could wrap himself, squatting to keep warm. He wore leather sandals, secured by straps around his ankles, and, around his head, a band with the appropriate decorations to show his status. His defensive armament consisted of a circular shield about 20 inches in diameter made of one or two layers of tanned leather, usually deerhide, although pigskin from the peccary may sometimes have been used. Although several parade shields consisting of cane covered with feathers exist, there is only one of the normal shields carried by warriors still to be found in the world, and this is in the Albert Memorial Museum at Exeter in Devon,

England. It is made of thick, well-tanned leather, and from the bottom half of it hangs a fringe of leather thongs, soft-tanned and about nine inches in length. The purpose of this fringe was to sweep away darts and spears.

A warrior usually carried one or two throwing spears of wood, with the blade edged with flakes or sharp stones, either chert or obsidian, which could inflict quite deep cuts on an enemy. In his right hand he carried a spear thrower, a wooden baton about 20 inches in length, with finger rings to give a secure grip at one end, and a hook at the other end which was engaged into the butt of a spear. This extended the length of the warrior's arm and gave greater leverage, so that his spear could be launched with great force against the enemy. As he advanced, leaping, singing, and whistling to terrify the foe, he would first throw darts with his spear thrower, and then resort to his Maquahuitl, a war club made of wood, about 30 inches in length, with grooved sides set with sharp flakes of obsidian. These are well known from drawings in the codices but no actual specimen appears to have survived. This was a deadly weapon, and with its aid great slices of flesh could be cut away from an enemy. To the Aztecs, it was a great misfortune if a wound was fatal as the enemy could not then be brought to the stone of sacrifice on the return of the victorious army. The Aztec warrior's equipment, although simple, was formidable and thoroughly adequate for native warfare. Ultimately, however, it failed to make any impression at all against the armoured Spaniards, although it wrought havoc among their Tlaxcalan Indian allies.

The armament of the warriors, and the structure of the army was very similar in the various centres of

ancient Mexican civilization. Frescoes at Teotihuacan in the early centuries of the Christian era show warriors with much the same equipment as the Aztecs in the early part of the sixteenth century. Toltec equipment in the tenth century was identical in every way to that of the Aztecs, except that Toltec warriors wore a wooden throat shield, and used a round kidney-shield decorated with various semi-precious stones. In some areas, and at some periods, special coats made of hardened leather were worn, which gave considerable protection even from the more deadly weapons. They are to be found represented in sculpture over the whole period from the time of Teotihuacan right through to the collapse of the Aztec empire.

There seems to have been no incentive to change a successful type of equipment or to invent anything which might prove to be more effective in battle. In

Above: An incense burner made of painted pottery in which incense or occasionally black rubber was burnt while the priest waved the bowl through the air. Slits on the side of the bowl allowed air to pass through so that the contents burned faster and produced more smoke. The symbol of the Smoking Mirror is painted on the top of the handle, while the handle as a whole is in the form of another symbol of Tezcatlipoca, the turkey claw

Left: Aztec noblemen often carried finely decorated equipment during ceremonies. On this turquoise encrusted wooden shield, the faces of the two warriors marching into battle are carved from shell. This was probably Mixtec craftsmanship, paid in tribute to the Aztecs

siege warfare there was no attempt to make huge covering shields such as were used by the Assyrian armies, or to invent a *ballista*. This illustrates the inherent distrust of innovation in ancient Mexico—all that existed was the will of the gods.

Being a warrior was the normal way of life for Aztec men, but, though it was nothing special, it gave opportunities which could bring an individual to great heights of glory and power, whatever his original social standing. If he succeeded in capturing three enemy soldiers single-handed and bringing them to be sacrificed, he was honoured as a Tequihua, or Master of Cuts. From this honour, which to judge from the paintings few ever achieved, he could go on to command larger and larger numbers of men. The higher echelons of the army were traditionally controlled by nobles of high ancestry, but the Great Speaker could allow an unusually astute and skilful soldier to enter their ranks. The young man would be given lands and allocated servants to till the land and to build him a small palace. He lived in state and was marked as a great warrior by the patterns on his cloak and by the kind of head-dress and lip-plug which he was entitled to wear. Thus, by the chances of war, a young man might rise from the masses into the orders of the nobility.

The training grounds of the army were organized within large courtyards, usually attached to the palaces in the city. There, the young men learnt the rigours of personal combat. The warriors would run forward screaming and waving their war clubs, clash their shields together, and, while each tried to push down the other's guard, attack each other with the clubs. The main purpose was to weaken the enemy so that he could not fight efficiently, and could be lassoed and then tied into a bundle which was carried out of the battle on the victor's back. In such wars there must have been continual processions of warriors coming up to fight in the front and then withdrawing with opponents bundled up on their backs while the next line of combatants engaged.

The organization behind all this was highly competent. The Great Speaker of the tribe was also commander in war. He gave general orders for a campaign, and, on important occasions such as his inauguration, he would lead the army himself. There were several grades of commanders in battle, of which the most important were marked by the great clusters of pendant feathers from their head-dress and their gloriously decorated cloaks. On the back of each commander a standard, rather like a tall, narrow flag, was fixed to mark his rank and serve as a rallying point for the warriors under his command. From accounts by the Spanish conquerors it is clear that many of these army commanders were carried on litters on the shoulders of a group of strong young men, so that they towered above the army and could be seen easily.

61

Left: Among the most important pieces of the Aztec warrior's equipment was his Atlatl or spear thrower. The two shown here are carved with scenes involving gods, warriors and sacrifices, and are covered in gold. The one on the right still retains the finger-grip made of clam shell. The detail shows a back-view: the groove into which the spear was slotted is terminated in the head of a god which covers a small hook. The hook was inserted into the butt of the spear handle, so that when the Atlatl was swung its effect was to extend the arm of the warrior and to fling the spear at great speed

Below: Back shield from Chichen Itzá worn by a Toltec nobleman and decorated with turquoise, red shell and lignite, representing the Feathered Serpent, the symbol of Toltec royalty

Aztec warriors were divided into two groups. Each was considered of equal importance and was symbolized by a sacred creature of combat, the eagle or the ocelot. The function of ocelot warriors was to reconnoitre before battle commenced; they would quietly range into the hills signalling to one another by imitations of the calls of birds and animals. Their purpose was to discover the disposition of the enemy force and to find strategic positions from which flanking attacks could be mounted. When their intelligence work was over they would rest for the night, since under normal circumstances no Mexican warrior would engage in a night attack. At dawn the eagle warriors would advance towards the enemy, as if they were mounting a frontal attack, chanting and stamping their feet. Then, as they prepared to charge, they let out powerful whistles by putting two fingers in their mouths and blowing with

all their might. This noise was supposed to represent the whistling of war darts and to intimidate the foe. As soon as the main bodies were engaged the ocelot warriors on the flanks would begin their attacks. Once they showed any sign of success the commander would release detachments from the rear of the main body to help the flanks and so gradually encircle the enemy force. Eventually the number of enemy captives would be considered fully sufficient and the commander of the enemy force was called upon by heralds to submit.

The priests as well as the warriors took a great part in war. Some carried smoking incense in among the soldiers as they chanted the praise of the gods, and urged the warriors to great efforts. Others actively took part in combat, claiming any prisoners for the service of their own temples.

Festivals of war

During the year there were a series of great festivals dedicated to the spirits of war. They were specially celebrated on that side of the great temple at Tenochtitlan (Mexico City) dedicated to Tezcatlipoca and his lieutenant Ixtilton—the Little Black One. These were the primary spirits of war and the inspiration of the warriors, so their festivals had to be as glorious and as bloody as possible.

These ceremonies occurred mainly in the summer and autumn, although one of the greatest was celebrated at the beginning of winter. This was Panquetzaliztli, the 'lifting of banners', which took place in the last days of November and the first part of December to honour Tezcatlipoca as Huitzilopochtli, the patron god of the Aztecs. The position of the stars marking the advent of this great festival were Aldebaran in Taurus, visible at midnight very high in the sky, and the star Regulus in Leo, equally high when the sun rose. In the evenings the constellation Aquarius was a sign that the power of the war gods was passing for a time, and that that of the fertility gods was about to come. During the great festival there were elaborate dances of warriors in their greatest finery clashing their shields, face to face in mock combat amid a blaze of golden ornaments, and red, yellow and green feathers. The captives to be sacrificed on this occasion had their hands dipped in blood and the handprints were pressed on the doorways of the temple just before they were stretched on the sacrificial stones.

The new year for the warriors began with a period of Toxcatl, from May 5 to 22 in the Western calendar. This means 'the slippery period', because the first rains had come, and the dust which had accumulated during the winter made the roads slippery. The festival was dedicated to the great god Tezcatlipoca, especially in his form as Huitzilopochtli. Once again, there were sacrifices of captured warriors. Important noblemen led by the high priests dressed in the insignia of the gods

Right: This page from the Codex Fejervary-Mayer *shows Tezcatlipoca, again identified by his missing foot, and his essential connections with war and sacrifice. He is surrounded by dates, showing his power over the 13-day periods of the Aztec calendar. The god is eating the palm of a sacrificed prisoner, a delicacy reserved for the highest nobility*

Below: Handle of a sacrificial stone knife. The blade would have been of carefully flaked chert (a coarse flint) and was extremely sharp, so that the victim's breast could be torn open and the still beating heart removed, almost as one action. Its gruesome purpose did not prevent the knife from being an exquisite object. This handle is of wood encrusted with turquoise and coloured shell, and represents a kneeling deity

danced before the people, and the legends of the gods were retold in mime with musical accompaniment.

The next important festival for the war gods was Tlaxochimaco, the 'coming of flowers', which lasted from July 22 until August 10. There were feasts of turkey and maize cakes in honour of Huitzilopochtli, for in one of his aspects the god appeared as the 'jewelled turkey' and indicated the course of the coming year. At this ceremony the priests sat round a bowl of finely ground maize flour in the temple, until, apparently miraculously, the footprint which symbolized Tezcatlipoca, the dreaded turkey claw, appeared. From its shape and position the priests were able to prophesy the year's events. This great public festival was a dance in which both men and women could take part and on this occasion the men were allowed to touch the hands of the women whom they faced in the dance.

At the end of August, and during the first part of

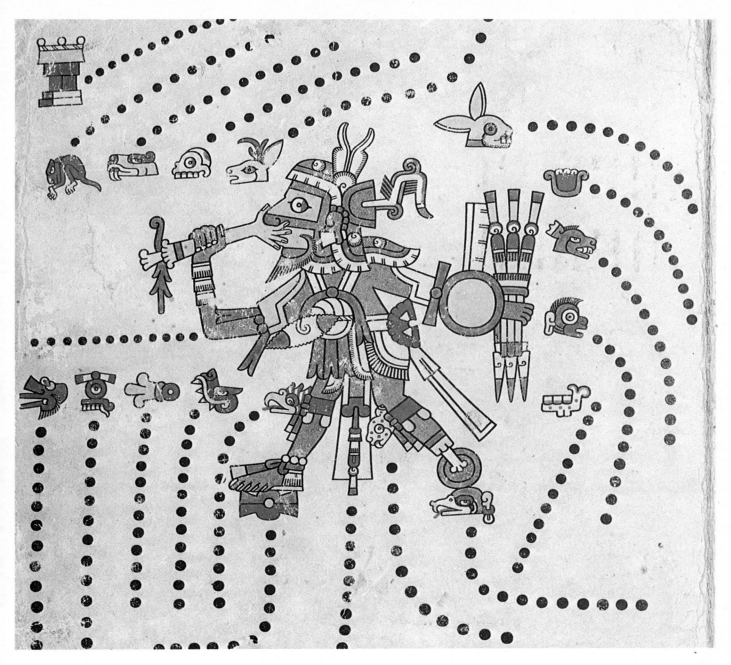

September, came the 'feast of the brooms', Ochpanitztli, in which there was a distribution of honours—special feathers, special dresses, nose-plugs, and so on—to the most important warriors. There were mock battles between the ocelot and eagle groups of warriors. The dances and the spectacle were dedicated to the goddess of grandmothers, Teteoinnan, whose function on this occasion was to prepare the warriors and brave men as fitting ornaments for the appearance of her son Tezcatlipoca, at the next festival. This was a harvest festival, Teotloco, held during the end of September and the early part of October, when Tezcatlipoca was believed to lead a great procession of gods who returned to earth after a sojourn in the skies. To celebrate this event the temple priests paraded through the town dressed as the gods.

The next festival of war was Quecholli, the 'small bird', which took place in the first 18 days of November.

This festival was dedicated to the hunting god Mixcoatl and people were expected to spend their spare time preparing weapons: flaking obsidian for spear heads, fashioning blades for the edges of the war clubs, making arrows, and performing acts of penance, all during the first four days of the period. There was some ceremonial hunting, and old people in particular were expected to refrain from all pleasures. Apparently this was a magical practice intended to ensure that the hunters and warriors, who would use the newly prepared weapons, would not be afflicted by the uncertainties and weaknesses of old age. This festival was the last before Panquetzaliztli, the lifting up of banners, which completed the circuit of the festivals of the war gods.

From the middle of December until the beginning of May there were no festivals concerned with warfare, although this was the period of driest weather, with occasional outbreaks of cold winds from the north,

65

and would appear to be particularly suitable for military expeditions. From the religious point of view, however, this period was not favoured by Tezcatlipoca, the god of war.

Sacrifice

The gods demanded various sacrifices: a few demanded slaves, while others demanded female victims, although women were never used for heart sacrifice but were usually strangled. The important sacrifices to the sun and to the war gods were all of male captives taken in war.

The prisoners to be sacrificed were not badly treated. They were marshalled back to the victorious town, manacled like slaves. Their wounds were attended to, and as soon as they were fit they were put into strong wooden cages so that they could not stand upright. The purpose was not to keep the prisoners uncomfortable,

but merely to prevent them from either escaping or taking exercise. They were fed with choice foods and generally well looked after. The purpose of this was to fatten them up since their limbs were later cut into tiny pieces and given to the people to eat. Hence, a fat prisoner was something of an asset.

On some of the great festivals, volunteer victims were painted to resemble the gods. In the midsummer festival the victim was dressed as the god Tezcatlipoca, and given four wives and the right to take anything he wished on his processions around the city. Eventually, however, his end was the same, a sudden sharp pain and the release of his soul to the paradise of the sun god.

It sometimes happened that there was a period in which no war took place, and no prisoners were taken for sacrifice. At such times the rulers of neighbouring cities would arrange a 'war of flowers'. Each side would bring a number of men to a pre-arranged battlefield,

Above: The only Aztec temple to survive the Spanish conquest and the subsequent destruction is in Santa Cecilia near Mexico City (Tenochtitlan). On the platform at the top of the steps is the god-house which would have contained images of the gods, and the entrance is flanked by two bowls in which fires would have been kept alight all night. Sacrifices were performed on a slab of stone in front of the god-house. When the heart had been removed and offered to the god the body was rolled away so that it tumbled down the steps. This must have softened the flesh so that it was easier to eat. Only the limbs were cannibalized; the remainder of the body was often fed to animals and the head was preserved for the skull rack

where they would have the opportunity of struggling for victory and taking the prisoners necessary for the sacrifices. Had this not been done, the gods would have been deeply offended. They would have plagued the people responsible for the lack of heavenly food by causing a drought or a storm, so that the welfare of the tribe would be seriously threatened.

The cult of the warriors was important politically, but it is doubtful if any Aztec thought of it simply in that way. They would be much more likely to think of the taking of prisoners and their eventual sacrifice as part of the law of nature. There are no statistics about the number of people sacrificed to the gods in ordinary times in Mexico, but in a small town probably about 30 people would be slain in a year, and in a tribal capital about 400. This, of course, excludes any crazed excesses like that perpetrated by the Aztecs when they dedicated the great temple in Tenochtitlan. In this case, 20,000 individuals were slain, the whole manpower of three Mixtec tribes from the mountains of Oaxaca.

It was not normally considered right to take human life, but sacrifice was necessary to placate the gods and to ensure the continued gifts of food and life. In any case, the soul of a sacrificial victim was sure of a glorious continued life in the heavens. Whether this hope of heavenly reward was sufficient to encourage captive warriors to face their doom with complacency is, of course, unknown, but, as with all human beings, the mystery of death is a very important factor in behaviour in life.

The making of an empire

The Aztec delight in war was not unnatural in such a strongly male-dominated society. One may parallel this attitude of mind with the behaviour of many nations of modern times. In the sphere of the American Indians, warlike activities characterized people of all types and levels of culture, from the sea-borne raids of the Indians of north-western America, to the expression of similar ideals among the greater tribes of the prairies after they had acquired the horse. The Aztec attitude differed only in their formal organization of warfare. As we have said before, the tactics were so arranged that a battle became almost a dance in honour of the gods of war.

As the empire grew, the Aztec army had to march further afield, beyond the valley of Mexico, and they occasionally found themselves travelling a thousand miles each way on a campaign, especially on those which led them into the mountains of what is now Guatemala. Mountain warfare, which in any case was normal in a rugged country like Mexico, could involve many extraordinary activities. To take a body of many thousands of men from the high plateau down through river valleys, across ravines, and up to other peaks and

67

passes, and then to continue the process day after day for many weeks before attacking an enemy ensconced in a town, fortified by a stone wall and itself high in the mountains, was a very difficult task. Although supplies might be obtained from villages *en route* the greater part of the rations of the warriors consisted of dried meat and flat wafers of corn bread called *tortillas,* which were carried on their backs. On the march they seized occasional flocks of turkeys, or shot a deer or a hare, but this was just a fortunate addition to the commissariat. Much of the cooking was done by the women who marched with the warriors. Additional sandals and bundles of arms were carried by women, and also by bands of teenage boys who did this work as part of their education in the art of war.

Sometimes, tragedy would strike, as in the case of 16,000 men who were drowned in a ravine as a result of a freak cloudburst. This occurred early in the reign of the last Aztec Great Speaker, Montezuma, in the mountains of Michoacan. Distant warfare was not always accompanied by triumph, and usually a small percentage of people died during the march, but the army normally reached its objective and defeated the enemy, either in battle or in siege warfare, without a great deal of difficulty. Sometimes they suffered fairly heavy casualties at the hands of mountain tribes who knew exactly where to create avalanches of rocks upon the ascending invaders. In the usual course of events, however, the town chief realized that the Aztec armament was superior, and surrendered, hoping that the terms would be reasonable.

Both commanders would meet and hold a long discussion. The Aztecs would explain that, since the enemy had disobeyed the instructions of their Great Speaker, the whole population should become slaves as well as paying tribute to the Aztecs. The other chief argued his own case as well as possible, and the normal outcome was an agreement that twice a year the conquered tribe would pay tribute when the Aztec tax collectors came to them. Since there was no money, the tribute comprised mainly local products of high quality. Several thousand blankets and a quantity of gold dust were normal requests, though in the south tribute was exacted in the form of bundles of coloured feathers and balls of raw rubber. Sometimes the southern area would also have to contribute bundles of vanilla pods and, even more importantly, packets of cacao beans from which 'chocolatl' would be made. These cacao beans were considered tribute of great value to the Mexicans. Two small hampers would purchase a male slave. Some of the mountain peoples would have to pay their tribute in the form of beads of green jade which came right across southern Mexico from the distant mountains of Guatemala.

In their unceasing drive for territorial power, the Aztecs had no conception of administering a newly conquered district for the benefit of the inhabitants. They were concerned merely with the quantity of plunder which could be brought back to Tenochtitlan, their great city in the lake, and as a result the population of Mexico came to hate their Aztec masters. It was no accident, then, that when the Spaniards arrived many of the subject tribes were willing to join them in the hopes that the hated Aztec rulers could be dispossessed. The failure of the Aztecs to create anything like a feudal system, in which there were reciprocal rights between each section of the population, led to a situation in which every subordinate tribe hoped that they could one day revolt and in turn establish themselves as masters of a predator state. Thus the cult of war attributed to Tezcatlipoca would certainly have destroyed the civilization in time. For a time it had been triumphant, with the fall of the Toltecs and the terrible interregnum of inter-city wars finally leading to the rise of the Aztecs.

Looking back to the time of the Toltec kings, before the demonic Tezcatlipoca became dominant, one might expect to find a more peaceful period, but the picture is remarkably similar. From the best record of the Toltec rule, the paintings in the *Codex Vindobonensis Mexic. 1,* the story of the Toltec kings shows that only two of them did not capture cities to add to the empire. These were the second and the eighth to rule after the first Quetzalcoatl, but in both cases there are symbols for the 'war of flowers'. This indicates that the whole ceremonial attitude towards war was the same among the Toltecs as it was among their successors the Aztecs, five centuries later. In both cases the symbol for the 'war of flowers', two large war darts wrapped up in a bundle of cloth, indicates that the weapons of war were not in use. In both cases we find that the associated kings are recorded as being concerned with gambling, and the boards for the sacred game of Patolli are much in evidence in the paintings. There are two symbols of

war associated with the first of these kings, Xolotl, and as there are no conquests it seems probable that they represent the repulsion of some kind of attack from outside. The second king whose name appears to be Quetzalcoatl, is associated with no war symbols whatever. The symbol of Quetzalcoatl decorated for sacrifice occurs in the reign of both of these kings, and also a disc, probably a ball of rubber, is shown with flames issuing from it. Apparently this also represents part of the symbolism of the 'war of flowers'.

It is safe to say that the cult of the warriors was as characteristic of Toltec society as it was of the Aztecs. Although the patron god of the Toltecs was Quetzalcoatl, he did not entirely displace the great Tezcatlipoca. The two gods were both active in the minds of the Toltecs, just as much as they were within the Aztec theology, but their dominance in the social structure was apparently reversed.

The defeat of Tezcatlipoca

It is clear that the whole life of the country depended upon the balance of the forces controlled by Tezcatlipoca and those associated with Quetzalcoatl. Since in the great and terrible struggle which marked the end of the Toltec period Tezcatlipoca was victorious, this dark god was believed to be in command of the forces of the universe. War was the most wonderful thing offered to Tezcatlipoca by the Aztec people, and was rewarded by the god with continual victory and strength. The whole philosophy was based on the reciprocal exchange of gifts between mankind and the sun, and between mankind and the great Tezcatlipoca, who as the power of darkness, the shadow within mankind, was the opposite of the sun. There was always an element of terror within this worship; failing the proper sacrifice, not only would the sun stop in the heavens

70

was no idea of the gods destroying one another—they were equal and opposite aspects of the powers of existence, both of which must have their position. It could be thought of in the same way as the alternation of day and night; there was no question that one was better than another.

Hernando Cortes landed on one of the very few days in which it was possible for Quetzalcoatl to assume his proper power. Thus the circuit of fate was completed, and the patron god of the country, the Smoking Mirror, would have to submit before the new power of the Morning Star. The history of the conquest of Mexico is, very largely, an enactment of this myth. The Aztec armies fought the invader only when the Morning Star was invisible, otherwise they would take up defensive positions or retreat. In all these events, the reign of superstition determined the course of Mexican history.

It is quite clear that for Mexican minds history was predetermined, and the fate of the nations had been decided by the rhythm of time even before they had come into being. There is no doubt that this pessimistic acceptance of total subservience to the rule of the gods led to a great deal of bravery, but it also led eventually to the end of their civilization. The Spaniards, too, fought with a religious zeal, though it was ultimately their greed which led to open conflict with the Aztecs and the destruction of Tenochtitlan.

None of the Aztec wise men could have realized that the end would come so dramatically, at the hands of a strange, white-faced people from over the seas only 18 years after the Aztecs had attained the goal promised them by the god. At the time of their fall, the Aztecs were indeed rulers of Anahuac, and their last fight was a struggle of tremendous intensity in which the warriors counted the loss of their lives as the winning of a place in heaven; they fought furiously to the end for the sake of their beloved but terrible patron god.

because the terrible heat was not assuaged by the stream of blood, but the Aztecs would also have been false to the god who protected them and had given them victory in war. Their end would surely have come. Yet the Aztec wise men already knew that the future was doomed, because they realized that, once the power of Quetzalcoatl had returned to this earth and the Morning Star had become the ruling Lord, then the power of Tezcatlipoca would be shattered, and the ancient ways would come to an end.

There was much confusion at the time of the Spanish conquest, but it does seem that great numbers of the population were hoping that one day Quetzalcoatl would return and bring a régime of greater human kindness in which the sacrifice of fruit and flowers and self-sacrifice through the offering of a little blood would replace the constant terror of the sacrificial stone and the immolation of human beings. But there

The Ritual of Daily Life

Above: Stele from Santa Lucia Cozumahualpa showing a priest making a drink offering to the sun. This pre-Toltec work expresses a theme which runs throughout ancient Mexican history—the placation of the mighty sun through offerings and sacrifice. In their daily lives the Mexican Indians were constantly conscious of their dependence on the sun, wind and rain

Left: Mixtec figure of the powerful rain god, Tlaloc, to whom offerings were continually made so that he would send his messengers, the rain clouds, and bring fertility. His head-dress indicates his high rank among the gods

Maize, in ancient Mexico, was the staff of life; people could not survive without the grain, which could be dried in storehouses and used whenever needed. It was ground up and made into *tortillas,* which remain as popular in Mexico today. With this source of sustenance everybody felt safe, and though they grew many other plants and ate meat of various kinds, maize was always the main foodstuff. For that reason it became the most revered and sacred plant.

Maize and its products, as well as every other plant, were regarded as the children of Mother Earth. They were especially holy, and the earth itself, as the mother of mankind, was even more sacred. Nobody could own the earth. Therefore, each group of families within the tribe formed a division, called a Calpulli, for the purposes of land distribution. The Calpulli was almost an autonomous group within the tribe. It seems to have once had a totemistic basis, but by historic times this had become submerged, and the social structure of the Calpulli was based on its occupation of an area of land. Only the nobility of closely related families retained any vestige of the old society. The Calpulli of the nobles depended on their descent from a Great Speaker of the Aztec tribe. They decided when the land should be dug and on which days the crops were to be reaped, although these were subsidiary to their higher administrative and military duties. The Calpulli among the other Aztecs was an organization which had its headman and council. Women held no office in this male-dominated society, nevertheless they advised their husbands and sons, and so were able to exert a considerable unofficial pressure.

The most important duty of the Calpulli was the redistribution of land which occurred, at most, once every four years. The cultivated area, which had been worked until there were signs of the yield falling off, was burnt over. Another area, which had been left fallow for some eight years, was then divided. The plots

allocated to families were scattered about in the whole section of land. This was a wise provision, because it meant that everybody had an equal chance of farming a plot of richer or of less productive land.

When the land had been distributed by the council of the Calpulli, the spring sowing began. The men cut down any trees which had grown on the fallow land and burned them so that the ashes could be used as fertilizer. They then broke up the ground, by pushing in digging sticks, and levering up the soil. The women followed with hoes to break up the clods. When the fields had been prepared, the women went round with their hoes and dragged up the earth into small mounds in the top of which four holes were made with a digging stick. The women put one grain of maize in each hole, and covered it over with a quick flick of their sandals. This was done over the whole field, the maize hills being about 18 inches apart in any direction.

After the sowing there came a period in which the men took no part in the work in the fields. The labour was not terribly arduous and the women and smaller children camped in little brushwood huts beside the fields as the crops ripened. They were there to keep the animals away, and, even more importantly, to weed the ground. Thus, everybody accumulated a basic store of food which could probably see the entire society through difficult times.

Most of the Mexican people had no idea that any secular activity would promote the fertility of their crops. They accepted the bounty of nature with thankfulness, offering their blood and even their children to the gods for the sake of life and fertility. Very few practised any kind of irrigation, although they did fertilize their fields. Slime from the lakes was used, and there were also traders who took large wooden canoes through the city in which they collected all the faeces and urine from the householders. The urine was kept separate in large jars and later used by the weavers for

Above: Panels from the Codex Fejervary-Mayer *representing, from right to left, the all-important fortunes of the maize plant over a four year period, indicated by the day symbols within each panel. On the far right the water goddess is shown in her form as a storm goddess, and the hand projecting from her head pours storm waters onto the maize which is shown as a healthy, strong plant, rooted in soil totally saturated with blue water. The following year is not so fortunate. At the top are signs showing cloudy days and clear, cold nights. The maize is now under the rule of the Lord of Jewels and is in poor condition, rooted in earth so dry that the digging stick, shown just in front of the plant, is broken. The third panel shows a year when Tlaloc is dominant and blesses the maize by making the earth rich and green. The digging stick is no longer broken and the plant is shown as Chalchihuitlicue, Tlaloc's young consort. The last panel, on the left, shows the bitter year when Xipe Totec rules the maize. The plant has failed to take root in the dry earth and is attacked by birds and animals. The four fates suffered by the maize have a calendrical significance and also express the concept of the four directions*

Right: Small pottery figurine in Olmec style, probably representing a fertility goddess. Around her neck she wears a shell pendant, and the entire figure was once painted red

bleaching their cloth. The faeces were heaped into the canoes and later dug out and scattered on the fields so that there was human manure for the growing plants. Manuring was haphazard and even this was meant as a religious offering of human waste.

The temple books clearly convey the idea that once in every four years there was likely to be drought and destruction. There are pictures showing the failure of rain and the coming of insects and destructive animals which attack the crops. On such occasions the people had no reservoirs of water to irrigate their fields and little to do except offer more blood and hope that the gods would relent. They had to resign themselves to eating just enough to avoid absolute starvation.

Once every autumn, the Great Speaker, as leader of the nation, opened the storehouses in which tributes of grain and dried food of many kinds had been kept. The contents were distributed to the people, but this was not always sufficient in times of drought. Some people tried to migrate at these times, although they usually died on the journey. Others sold themselves into slavery to great lords, whose fields were thought to have good supplies of grain which could be given to their servants. This must always have been hard on these individuals, since the Aztecs were passionately jealous of their independence. Yet, against the risk of starvation, there was little else that could be done. The farmer simply had no means of controlling the fertility of his soil or the safety of his crops. In times of drought, plagues of mice left their accustomed haunts and raided the fields in search of food. Insects flourished, and laid their eggs in the growing plants. The dusty heat, with the prospect of starvation and a miserable death, overshadowed the whole population. Celebrations for the gods were held and sacrifices were made. It was generally accepted that mankind had saddened the gods and that the drought was a punishment.

The farmer was not only the support of the nation,

but also the slave of the gods. He did what he could to bring life and food for his people, but was always aware that the forces of drought and disaster might bring destruction. This is vividly illustrated in many Mexican religious codices, particularly in the long document *Vaticanus 3773*. Even at the worst of times, however, the people knew that disaster and death would eventually give way to life, fertility and happiness.

One of the great problems of the Aztec farmer was the growth of population. There seems to have been no great epidemic once the tragedies that followed the fall of the Toltecs were over, and even the endemic warfare and the regular practice of human sacrifice did little to restrict the growth of population. It has been suggested that a people's fertility increases when they are living on the edge of hunger, and this may well be true. Certainly, all the time that the small Aztec tribe was growing into a powerful nation, there was a

Above: Bas relief showing Tlaloc, the rain god, bringing blessings to the maize goddess. Each deity holds a maize plant with ripened cobs towards the other

Right: Pre-Toltec stone column from Atzcapotzalco showing the face of Tlaloc, with projecting teeth and a tongue in the form of a maize plant. At the top of the column, which would probably once have been in a priest's house, is the symbol of water bringing fertility

steadily increasing pressure on local food resources. The political failure to amalgamate different tribes into a nation made it difficult, if not impossible, for tribes to share out available resources, and each group was restricted to its own territories.

Hunters and gardeners

The most interesting agricultural advance by the Aztecs was due to the rapid expansion of their population, which forced them to expand the possibilities of their rocky islets in the midst of the lake. They began to extend their land area by putting up rough fences of basketry in the lake, onto which they piled mud and soil dredged from the bottom. After a while this reclaimed soil became very fertile. As each patch came into cultivation, further land was added, always leaving waterways between the new areas. The use of shrubs and trees for consolidating the ground was probably accidental, though the Aztecs loved the shade of the trees and their beautiful flowers and fruit. The cultivation of Chinampas, as these 'floating' gardens were called, extended in all directions between the five great causeways which linked Tenochtitlan with the mainland. Farther out in the lake the Aztecs built a great stone barrier to stop storm waves flooding over into the water of the city. On one side was the deeper lake and on the other the shallow, muddy waters on which more and more Chinampas were being built. Nowadays the only remainder of this is to be found in the extreme south of the lake, where the canals and gardens of Xochimilco remain, not only as the suppliers of flowers to the city, but also as pleasure gardens. A great part of the population of Mexico City finds this a most agreeable area for relaxation on Sunday afternoons. As in ancient days, the land is rich and the mud from the bottom of the canals is being continually dredged up and put on the land. It is ideal for the intensive flower planting which is its characteristic today, as much as it was in the past. The Aztecs were always extremely fond of flowers, and men of distinction used to walk through the city carrying little nosegays of the most beautiful blooms that could be found.

Gardens close to the houses were used for growing vanilla orchids, and also one or two highly valued varieties of pepper. Several varieties of melon and gourd were also grown in large quantities, especially in the rich soil of the Chinampas. In the woodlands, which were not then as widespread as they are today, people would gather nuts and berries, not in great amounts, but sufficient to make a change in the regular diet. A few root crops such as camotes, a yam-like vegetable, were regularly grown and provided rather solid, stodgy food.

The leaves of some wild plants were edible, and

Left: *The beautiful gardens of Xochimilco, to the south of Mexico City. These gardens are all that remain as a reminder of the Chinampas, the Aztec 'floating' gardens. The land is constantly replenished with soil dredged from the bottom of the lake and is extremely fertile. Chinampas surrounded the Aztec capital, Tenochtitlan, and were used mainly for growing the flowers which were in constant demand among the noblemen of what was then one of the largest cities in the world. Between the gardens were canals, thronged with the canoes which brought trade and the spoils of war to the Aztecs at the height of their power*

were sometimes cultivated for that purpose. There were also certain mosses that grew on trees which could be dried and included in stews. Several varieties of mushrooms were known which could be cooked and eaten with impunity. This was reasonably safe, since the Aztecs had made a truly scientific study of the botanical wealth of their country, and the properties of plants.

The magic mushroom was used in some religious or medicinal ceremonies. It provided no nourishment since it caused violent vomiting which emptied the stomach, but its main purpose was hallucinogenic. By releasing tensions in the unconscious mind, it induced what were thought to be visions of reality, but it remained a carefully guarded property of the priesthood and was used only for religious purposes.

Cakes made of amaranth seeds were used in the festivals for Huitzilopochtli. They were modelled in the shape of figures of the god, and put up on high poles which the young men then climbed in an effort to pull them down as trophies. Similar cakes were also eaten at some of the greater ceremonies for the gods, and were particularly important in the worship of the rain gods.

The food reserves available to the Aztecs were not limited entirely to agricultural produce and wild plants. Water birds were caught in nets hoisted on poles by bird catchers, who hunted in pairs. In the houses, most families kept turkeys, and these flocks, although small in number, provided a rich part of the diet. The cock turkey was looked on with some awe since a special variety, with a blue wattle, was thought to be the emblem of the god Tezcatlipoca. The pride of the displaying turkey was supposed to reflect the personal glory of this god, and its gobbling was believed to represent his voice.

Fish from the lake were commonly eaten in Tenochtitlan and occasionally relays of runners from the sea coast brought baskets full of fish packed in seaweed into the city. This was a difficult task and such rare delicacies were reserved for the nobles and the ruling group who occupied the palaces in the heart of the city. On the lake, the Aztec fishermen used individual nets and also small seine nets drawn between two canoes. The boys and young men occasionally cast darts from their throwing sticks to impale particularly large and succulent fish, though probably mainly for sport. Their knowledge of the natural history of the lake was very considerable, and the Aztecs named many varieties of edible and useful fish as well as classifying many other creatures.

Mice, voles, very small serpents and frogs were not unwelcome sources of food, and were, indeed, very palatable when cooked in an earth oven. An armadillo cooked in its shell produced a tasty meal. Dogs, especially a variety of Tepeitzcuintli, the Mexican hairless dog, were fattened for food and must have looked like waddling water melons. When cooked they were said to be exceedingly succulent, and the Spanish conquerors often found them an invaluable food. They also used the fat from these dogs for cleaning out wounds instead of the oil and vinegar treatment more common in Europe at that time. The nets in which these animals were trapped were made out of beaten roots of trees, often from varieties of pine and cedar, the commonest trees in the mountains. In the areas close to the towns, the maguey cactus provided sisal fibre which is still used for making ropes.

In the mainland villages there were herds of semi-domesticated pigs. These were wild peccary which had been caught as piglets. Although treated very kindly as piglets (some of them were even breast-fed by the women for a time), they usually developed a surly ferocity, characteristic of their kind. Thus, a herd of pigs, even though belonging to only one of the village Calpulli, could become the subject of general hunting rather than slaughtering. The meat was, of course, excellent, and the strong bones provided material for weapons and tools. The hide, carefully cured by greasing and smoking was very useful for sandal thongs, straps for the back-packs in which burdens were carried, and also for forming the faces of the shields carried by the warriors.

In the forests of Mexico there were large herds of wild deer which were preserved with great care. During Aztec times they became scarce, so that hunting was very strictly controlled. At the proper season the Great Speaker of the Aztecs declared a general hunt. Beaters were sent into the wood, and the noblemen killed the deer with spears and darts thrown from their spear throwers. The products of the hunt were never sufficient for more than one or two festival meals, and these were normally the prerogative of the ruling class. It appears that at the same time, however, village hunts were

permitted in which small numbers of deer were killed and eaten by the villagers at special festivals. Deer hunting was more important in the hills of Tlaxcala, where Camaxtli, the Deer God, was especially revered, and hunting normally formed a greater part of the economy than among the Aztecs. The Tlaxcalans had the reputation of being a comparatively primitive people and they were usually allowed to flourish in their own way unless the Aztecs had taken insufficient prisoners in war to sacrifice to the gods. In this case, Tlaxcalan towns and villages were attacked and the young men were carried off. This proved to be most unwise, because, once the Spaniards arrived, the Tlaxcalans joined with them in attacking Tenochtitlan. The Tlaxcalan forces proved to be a major factor in the final destruction of Aztec power, since they provided carriers and warriors in sufficient numbers to enable Cortes to finally capture and destroy the great city.

Agricultural festivals

It was believed that humanity and the gods were part of an eternal state of being. There seems to have been no trace of a desire to improve agricultural yields, to introduce irrigation, or in any way to suggest that mankind had any relationship to food production other than digging and planting at the prescribed times. For how long this simple agriculture and its range of ceremonies had continued unaltered is unknown to us, but 5,000 years would seem to be a conservative estimate. The recordings in the temple books gave such strength to the fatalistic traditions that any important individual contributions were inhibited. Naturally this inhibition, this feeling of being enslaved to fate, intensified the reactions of the priests who impersonated the gods at the festivals and they reached an ecstatic state in which the atrocities of human sacrifice became an essential part of life.

All life involved a certain degree of hardship. Among the puritanical Aztecs happiness was always thought to be vaguely improper, although, of course, they experienced their times of joy and contentment. Nevertheless, the atmosphere of the civilization was one in which mankind was always in awe of the gods, always in a state of doubt as to what fate might bring. In spite of all the efforts to predict fate, through the magical books and the stars, there was uncertainty built into the system itself. This was probably at its height among the Aztec intellectual groups when, every 52 years, the period came in which the sun god and his powers might become servants of a returned Quetzalcoatl, instead of Tezcatlipoca.

For most of the farmers of Mexico, the more abstract features of the gods were important only in a distant sense. The immediate concern was their need for help from all forces of the natural world. The water goddess was obviously very important to them, for in this dry country, they relied on the rivers and springs to keep the ground moist between the storms of the rainy season. The winds which dried the ground for planting and carried the rain clouds were equated with Quetzal-coatl as Ehecatl.

There was the great lady under the earth, Coatlicue, who made the plants grow, though when it came to such a vital plant as maize, there was a series of goddesses and finally a god who represented the maize throughout the stages of growth. Similarly there were spirits who looked after all other living things. These not only included the spirits of the dead appearing as butterflies, but also lesser creatures, more of the quality of fairies in European folklore. They were visible in little whirl-winds of dust in the dry season, or in the sudden and unexpected movement of leaves of plants in still, hot weather. For the farmer, the whole universe was alive, and sentient, though he could not expect these powers to help unless he made occasional small offerings. Some articles of food were left for these spirits, and a few drops of blood were thrown in the direction where they were supposed to take their abode, in the hope that the spirit world would help in growing food. These nature gods were not thought to be willing to take the regular routines of work as their due, but they expected an offering of life's strength, of blood, sometimes of human sacrifice. Nature gave so much that everybody could understand how it could best be repaid. Even the sacrifice of a child was small when compared to the benefits that were given to the whole of the family by the growing crops and the spirits that protected them. This shows an utterly unscientific attitude, but then the ancient Mexican did not consider that he could regulate the powers of nature without spiritual assistance.

On the occasion of the great festivals which took place, one for each 20 days of the year, the farming family would go to the village temple, or even to the great city,

Above: Aztec standing figure of Xochiquetzal, the flower goddess regarded as the patron of all flowering plants. A quetzal bird forms part of her head-dress and quetzal feathers fringe her garments. The pendant around her neck carries the symbol for gold, while her nose-pendant displays her high rank. In her left hand she holds a small bunch of flowers

Left: Aztec stone carving depicting Xochipilli, the Lord of Flowers. He is shown singing and accompanying himself with a rattle in each hand, though the rattles are now missing. This happy, almost impudent figure is decorated with flowers, which had symbolic connections with the heat of the sun

where they would take part in the ceremonies by singing and dancing at the appropriate moment. They made little offerings of goods, and also took advantage of the occasion to bring goods for exchange in the market.

The year was filled with a sequence of festivals, the most important of which concerned the growth and development of the maize plant. The saddest of all these agricultural ceremonies was that held at the beginning of spring, the festival of Atlcoualo, when it was necessary to call for rain. This occurred in late February. Each district of the town, and each village would sacrifice a chosen child in a great ceremony of weeping. The selected child was taken in a carrier, decorated with reeds and symbols of the water spirits, to a nearby river. When the time came for sacrifice, the child was beaten so that it cried and all the people burst into tears, beating each other and sorrowing. The falling tears were supposed to encourage the rain gods to look down and take pity on the people, giving them the tears of water from the clouds. The child was then, with great ceremony, thrown into the water and drowned, and, to the accompaniment of great wailing, the people slowly returned. Black balls of rubber carried their smoky message to the skies and indicated to the rain gods that the clouds were expected and that rain should come. Although the people were not to know it, this time of the year naturally inaugurated a period of showery weather which was a presage of coming winds and then the rains of springtime. They naturally must have felt that their tragic offering was the cause of the gods relenting and bringing the blessing of rain.

Another piece of imitative magic took place at the festival called Tlacaxipeualiztli. A prisoner taken in battle was paraded around the town by his captor, and people made gifts of food and clothing. Then the prisoner was taken to the temple on the festival day in late March, and there dosed with drugs, and skinned alive. The powders which had been given and the

Top left: Rhythmic music was an essential feature of all the great festivals in ancient Mexico and a Teponaztli, or two-tone drum, provided the main rhythm. The drum was beaten on the two flaps, or tongues of wood, at the top. This Mixtec drum has been delicately carved in hardwood to depict a battle scene

Above: Small pottery whistles, used by Aztec dancers at festivals to mark time

Top centre: Typical Aztec flageolets, or small flutes. Investigations into the nature of ancient Mexican music have suggested a structure based on five tones

Top right: Pottery ocarina in the form of a turtle, the tail of which formed the mouthpiece

Right: Pottery figurine of a dancer at a festival, throwing his head back to sing. The face shows great tension, and is adorned with a lip-plug and ear-rings. The dancer is holding his loin-cloth as he dances

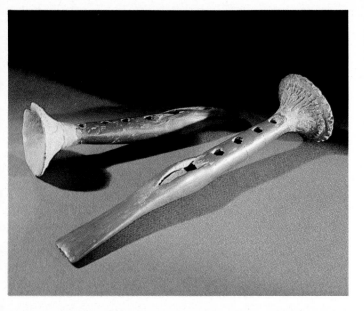

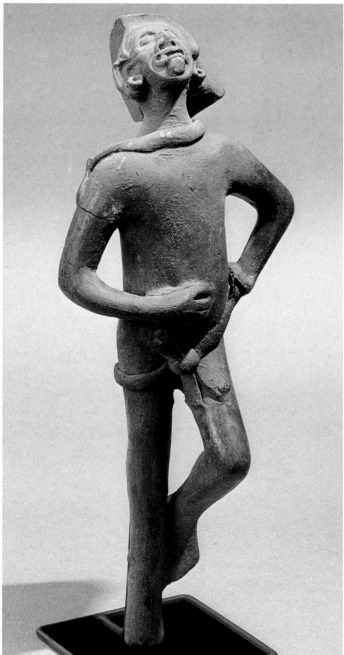

incense which was blown over him were intended to ease the pain of the scorching which preceded the skinning. Nevertheless, the victim was alive, even if only semi-conscious, while cuts were made around the neck, arms and legs, and down the back so that the skin could be ripped away from the body. The carcass, red and bleeding, was then thrown over the stone and the heart cut out. The heart was offered to the gods, and the skin was immediately put on by the warrior who had originally taken the victim prisoner. Dressed in this horrible garb, and wearing a mask made from the skin of the face of the victim, the warrior danced, waving his war club and crying to the heavens for new life and new strength.

After a few days, the dead skin would dry up, crack, and fall to pieces. In the process it had of course decomposed and the smell of the rotting flesh attached to it was thought to be disgusting even by the Mexicans, but they felt that the breaking of old skins must come to every seed of maize that they had planted. The young maize plant must force its green shoot from the apparently dead seed, bursting through the golden skin, just as the warrior burst out of the yellow skin of the dead man. So holy were these skins, that at the completion of the festival they were carefully gathered up and bundled, to be kept in a vault underneath a special temple of Xipe Totec, the god of suffering.

This ceremony sounds horrible to us, and apparently the Aztecs also considered it to be something which was shocking as well as noble. But to them it was a seal on the pact between mankind and the gods. Man gave suffering and pain, his own labour in the fields as well as the sacrificial victims to the gods, in return for the food which came from the young maize plants. There was no escape: the gods gave life, and the gods demanded a certain proportion of life in return.

The next festival, Tozoztontli, was again one of prayer for rain and this lasted from the end of March to

85

the middle of April. It was dedicated to the Earth Mother and to the rain spirits. This was followed by a long feast called Hueitozoztli, or the feast of the Xilotes, the young green maize plant, and the occasion was one of great rejoicing. There was dancing and singing and young people congregated to be happy together. The girls, once their breasts had developed, would normally keep them covered, but they now threw aside their capes. The idea behind the showing of breasts for the few days of the festival was certainly not a sexual one, but it was meant rather as a display of flowering beauty, and to the Mexicans it had the added and important connotation of food to come. The maize plants were producing the young green cobs. Before long these would become golden and ripe, and would bring food to the granaries of the nation. Therefore, the season must be one of happiness.

Nevertheless, at every important temple there had to be an offering of a woman to the maize spirits. Very often she was selected, but not told that she was going to be the victim. She was taken, mildly intoxicated, to dance with the priests in a happy ceremony. Suddenly, she was seized, cast over the back of one of the priests, and her head was sliced off. The blood, spurting in the four directions, was supposed to bring fertility to the crops of the whole nation. At this festival the blood-letting was general: everybody cut their ears, and men offered blood from holes pierced in their tongues. The underlying idea was to give blood as the life force to strengthen fertility, and to offer a woman, the source of life, to the spirit of the life of the maize plants.

There was then a pause in the agricultural festivals until the latter part of May and the first half of June, when the festival of Etzalqualiztli, which means 'bean porridge', began. The name referred to the semi-fasting of the period when rain was called for. There was a certain amount of human sacrifice to the rain spirits, and an amusing occasion in which young people ran through the town snatching everything that was lying about loose, as a symbol of the seizing of the corn cob that would come later when the fruit was ripe. This festival was followed by Tecuilhuitontli, the lesser feast of the Aztec lords. The last part of July was covered by this festival in which the salt workers were particularly honoured and salt was imported from the sea coasts.

Early in July, Hueitecuilhuitl, the greater feast of the lords, was held. At this time the maize was just becoming ripe, and there was a festival for Xilonen, who was the goddess of the young maize. For eight days the young women with their breasts bare and their hair down, impersonated the young goddess. After the sacrifice of a slave girl, people were allowed to eat some of the new unripe corn, which served as a kind of first fruit.

The harvest festival, Ochpaniztli, came in the first half of September. This was the most joyful of the Aztec festivals for it meant that the gods had rewarded

Right: Gold jewellery was frequently worn in ancient Mexico as ear and nose ornaments, necklaces, armlets and anklets. The greatest traditions of craftsmanship were among the Mixtecs, who supplied the Aztecs with much of their jewellery. This ear-ring is Mixtec work from Monte Alban and is composed of a gold skull from which hang tiny golden bells

Far right, above: Mixtec gold nose-pendant in the form of a bearded god with an elaborate head-dress

Far right, below: When attending festivals, the Aztecs wore face-paint and probably used small pottery stamps such as these to imprint patterns on their cheeks

Below: Necklace of hollow golden beads, modelled around clay which was then scraped out

the people with food, and life would continue. Five heads of maize, fully ripened, were carried to each household in honour of the Lady Chicomecoatl, whose name, literally interpreted, means seven serpents. Poetically, however, the serpents were thought of as something which came out of the ground, as magical beings living just under the surface of the earth. The name also referred to other things which came out of the earth, and, in this case, it was the maize plant. The goddess was thus honoured with a beautiful name, without our uglier connotations of the word 'serpent', and in art she was shown with five maize cobs in the headband which she wore.

Of course, there were sacrifices on this occasion, but the central ritual was the procession of dancing and singing as the ripe ears of corn were brought in from the fields. It was clear that the gods had willed that the people should eat for another year. The girls wore their

hair loose with bands of flowers. Young men dressed in their best loin-cloths, and with all their face paint and head-dresses showing their social achievements. They carried small, hollow gourds filled with flour, which they threw at the girls, spattering them with a creamy-white dust. Singing and dancing were universal and the whole city was given up to joy. The villages surrounding the lake similarly celebrated their happiness. The land, which had been blessed with fertility, was the goddess herself, the great Earth Mother. The people were her children and she had granted them happiness through her many assistants who had developed the life-giving maize.

The great festival for the rain gods, the Tlaloques, was the 'mountain feast', Tepeilhuitl. There were races up to the mountains, and figures of the gods were made and covered with a paste made from amaranth seeds, which were afterwards eaten. The next feast of the

Tlaloques did not come until December. This was Atemoztli, the falling of the waters. There were vigils to observe the winter solstice, offerings were made for the household gods, and poles were erected holding paper streamers, covered with rubber. This was because rubber, when burning, gave off clouds of black smoke and was believed to tempt the great storm clouds of the rainy season to come.

At the turn of the year came Tititl, the stormy weather. There were human sacrifices and people would weep in an attempt to make the rain fall more richly. Children were beaten with bags filled with flour, and women scratched themselves so as to make tears pour down their faces. This was to bring good luck for the rest of the year. The next period, which ran from mid-January to mid-February, was Izcalli, the 'house of stones', during which corn was dried and roasted. There was a ceremony for the fire god, and a ceremonial

Top left: Domestic pottery in ancient Mexico was hand-coiled, and not thrown on a wheel. These bowls are typical Aztec household ware, their scored interiors indicating that they were meant to be used for grinding peppers in the preparation of meals

Top right: Painted bowl standing on feet in the form of eagles' heads, which may indicate that the bowl was part of a warrior's household

Above: In later Aztec times the decorations on household pottery became more intricate. Bowls like these were made and decorated by women in the home

hunt. After this, at the beginning of February came five 'unlucky' days before the year started again with the festival of Atlcoualo.

The Aztec household

The gods were constantly revered within the family circle. The most sacred place in the home was a small fire which was kept going at the centre of the house. This was the shrine of Xiuhtecuhtli, the Lord of Fire and the earthly representative of the great Creator, Ometecuhtli, who lived beyond the Pole Star. Within the house, there was also a crib for the dried corn, in front of which stood a basket holding five sacred ears of maize, formed into the image of a woman and dressed accordingly. This represented the goddess of the maize, Xilonen, the fertility goddess who also looked after the health of the home. In other corners there were little clay, or rough stone, statuettes of gods. A favourite was that of a young man painted black, Ixtlilton, who was not only the lieutenant of the war god, but who also protected sleeping children. He was the darkness, and he brought peace over their eyes, and let them sleep happily, freeing them from the dread of any incursion of the ghosts and strange spirits living outside in the night.

In every way the gods reflected aspects of human beings in their passage through life. There can be no question that they represented what Jung called the archetypes. There were many of them: the teasing corn maidens—the spirit of life in the corn; the rain spirits—mischievous and powerful, givers of life; the great Earth Mother—the apotheosis of all successful femininity. There were also gods whose function was dangerous, and yet who represented youth, the eternal children of the universe. Thus, the gods were part of the nation, and of every individual family in that nation.

In the city the better houses were built of stone, but

Above: Aztec calcite vessel in the form of a hare. In the more affluent households vessels like this would have been used to hold cocoa, which was regarded as an aphrodisiac. The cocoa beans were ground, mixed with the gum of liquidambar trees and water, and were then drunk through straws made of gold

towards the outskirts more and more houses were made of cane plastered over with clay, with a thatch of palm leaves. These were cool, clean and rainproof. The thatch harboured many insects, but smoke from the small cooking fire in the room must have kept them down. People slept in the corners of the house, where a mat was laid down. There was usually only a cotton blanket as coverage, even in winter, so there was little extra warmth. The mats were placed so that the feet were closer to the central fireplace, and thus a little comfort was gained.

Often, not far from the house, usually in the courtyard, there was a small building about four feet high. This was the family sweat bath, which was, it seems, used in times of illness, or perhaps whenever the bather felt rather less healthy than usual. Prayers were first said to a little image of the Earth Mother, which was placed just over the doorway and a fire was made against the outside of the stone walls, so that the stones became very hot. The person going into the sweat bath took a bowl of water and some green twigs. The twigs were used to splash water against the hot wall. The building gradually became filled with steam, while the bather gently beat himself with the twigs. Then, when covered with sweat and gasping for breath, he burst out of the little doorway and dashed to the nearest pond or stream of cold water. On the whole, this treatment was invigorating and health giving, but in later times, after the Spanish invasion, it was used as a treatment for smallpox, and it probably accelerated the millions of deaths that took place at that frightful time.

Every morning, people looked out of their doorway to see if the Morning Star was in the sky. If it was, the ear was pierced with a cactus spine and two drops of blood were put on the fingers and thrown to the sky towards the Morning Star, so that Quetzalcoatl should have strength and life and give blessings. Every morning, each man knew the name of the day, and considered his fate as the sun rose. Every night brought fear, and people huddled indoors. Only the priests, and the boys training to be priests, dared to go out in the darkness, for the world was then full of ghosts and dreadful spirits which might seize anyone and bring them sickness or even death. Everybody, unless some very pressing duty kept them, went to bed early, usually immediately after sunset.

It seems that a girl's domestic duties would include rising very early with her mother and putting the grains of maize into water with a little lime mixed in with it, so that they could be left for a day to soften. Maize that had softened on the previous day was put on the stone slab called a metatl and crushed with a stone bar, until it became a smooth, even paste. This was allowed to dry for a minute, and then small lumps of it were beaten down on a stone slab over the fire. They dried and changed colour to a rather soft, golden brown. The end product was a *tortilla,* which was the staple food of the Mexican Indians.

Young girls wore their hair long, well-combed and usually glistening through constant oiling and combing. Married women plaited their hair and wrapped ribbons around two main plaits, which were arranged across the forehead with the ends standing up like horns on either side of the head. These represented the head-dress of the goddess Xochiquetzal and showed that the women desired many children. Both men and women wore ear-rings, very often of gold, and some men wore ornaments through the septum of their nose. Great noblemen would have their lower lip pierced, with a pendant hanging from it, and their ear-rings were often very large, glittering with gold and jade.

A man's basic dress consisted of a loin-cloth, and people of all ranks wore this with elaborately embroidered flaps in front and behind. All people wore sandals with straps of jaguar skin, and the Great Speaker wore golden sandals, although when he left his room in the palace his feet were never allowed to touch the ground. He was usually carried in a litter supported by the great military nobles of the empire. Most men had a decorated woven cape, which was tied in a knot on one shoulder, and this was usually brilliant in colour. Those who could afford it had it covered in fine featherwork.

Every woman wore a wrap-around skirt, tucked into a belt. Some of the wealthier women had little golden or bronze bells sewn all the way along the fringe of the skirt. The fringe was supposed to come just below the knee for the sake of decency, and the wearer had to walk with small steps so that the skirt would not open at the side and reveal her knees. Over the skirt she wore a Quexquimitl, a simple poncho with a central opening for the head. The edges were elaborately fringed and it was covered with bright patterns embroidered by the women. It was not considered at all proper for women to allow their breasts to be seen openly in public.

Men painted their faces in bands of black, white, blue, red, or whatever colour was proper for the occasion. Women usually painted their faces with yellow ochre, and on each cheek they would use a carved pottery stamp to impress a pattern in red cochineal. The effect would be startling to us, but they considered it beautiful.

Marriages were arranged through the parents of the two families who employed a 'marriage-broker' to arrange the necessary payment of a dowry. We might call it a bride-price, except that there was a similar price for the bridegroom. The bridegroom's family expected compensation for the loss of services of their son as wood-worker, cultivator, and possibly as a young warrior who had brought home plunder from the wars. The girl's family expected compensation for her possibilities as a weaver and as a maker of pottery, and as a woman who could bargain well in the market

Right: Aztec figure of a monkey holding a partially eaten fruit in one paw. On his chest is the Oyoualli, a symbol representing the female sex organs. This is typical of the way the Aztecs saw monkeys: as mischievous and lascivious creatures

Below: This picture from the Codex Becker *shows the marriage of a Mixtec couple of noble birth. Their names are indicated by the signs above their heads. The lady's plaited head-dress indicates her married status and the black footprints going up between them lead to a picture of their future children*

places. There was thus a great deal of haggling and argument before the marriage ceremony could take place.

The marriage itself was a very simple ceremony relying on a declaration of intent, often before a priest. Each of the young people wore a scarf for the occasion and the ends of these scarves were knotted together, symbolizing the union. The ceremony itself may have been simple, but it was surrounded by a great deal of speech-making by all the relatives on each side. This was thoroughly enjoyed since Nahuatl was a naturally poetic language, and all manner of similes and allusions were made by the speakers, so that each of the rather long speeches was likely to become an expression of poetic art in its own right. At the end of all the speech-making, which appears to have taken at least half a day, there was a festival in which meals were served. If the bridegroom discovered that his bride was not a virgin,

Above: Double staircase of the Aztec temple at Tenayuca. The form of this staircase is very similar to that on the great pyramid of Tenochtitlan, though much smaller. The god-house stood at the top of the stairway but it was made of wood and no longer exists

the *tortillas* would be served in baskets with no bottoms so that they fell in a heap and the whole party broke up in distress. So strict was Aztec training, however, that such a disgrace was an extremely rare event.

After a marriage the young couple were assisted by their relatives in house-building and furnishing. Every time a child was born, the grandparents would make little presents, which would always include a small jade bead and a green feather, as wishes of long life and protection from the gods. Children learned the usual conduct of life simply by living with their families and their neighbours, observing and doing what others did.

A favourite strong drink at weddings and on other festive occasions was called pulque. This was prepared by cutting out the heart of the maguey plant, sucking up some juice into a gourd, and then pouring it out into a storage bowl. The girls of the family would chew some of it, swilling it around their teeth, and spitting it back into the bowl. The ptyalin in their saliva acted as a fermenting agent, and after a few days the bowl of pulque would be frothing and smell really unpleasant. The froth was skimmed off the top, however, and the pulque was then tipped into small bowls to be passed around the family. It was quite a pleasant drink to taste, and people poured it down their throats quickly. If they drank too much, of course, they became intoxicated though it was not much stronger than a normal beer.

People who became drunk in public were threatened with the most severe penalties. A young man found drunk where he might possibly be seen by a stranger from another tribe would incur the death penalty. He had betrayed a weakness in the Aztecs and shown some way in which the Aztecs might have been defeated in war, and that could not be tolerated. Women who became drunk were likely to behave lasciviously, and so were thought of as immoral and beaten by their husbands. If they actually fell into a life of prostitution, they were attached to camps of young warriors. Whenever any signs of weakness or illness were discerned in them, they were taken away and strangled. Their bodies were thrown into the swamps, since they were considered quite unfit for normal sacrifice.

It is quite probable that the harsh morality of Aztec tradition gave rise to their peculiarly bloodthirsty type of religious worship, since, in a thoroughly Freudian sense, sex and cruelty are closely related. This is especially apparent in primitive society. Mexican men were expected to be faithful to their wives, and, for most men, sex was a normal, private affair. In the religious paintings of the Aztecs, sexual intercourse is usually shown by depicting the heads and feet of two people projecting from beneath a blanket. In some cases the people are drawn naked beside each other, but joined only by a red object in the shape of a stone knife between their mouths to indicate the joining of their tongues. In this austere and modest way, the giving of life from the gods, with all its possibilities of ecstasy, was reduced to a quiet, formal pattern. The reason may have been the need to hide from any stranger the fact that the Aztecs found any enjoyment other than in battle.

Merchants and markets

Not all parts of Mexico could produce the same materials, and the footpaths running over the mountains and forests were routes followed by bands of Pochteca, the name given to the merchants. The members of the merchants' societies were deliberately unostentatious and secretive. They did not wish to appear to be rich and tempt the noblemen to plunder them, and they did not wish the mass of people to learn how their trade goods were bargained for, or how their own secret

Below: Featherwork was a finely developed craft in Aztec times. This ornamental disc is an excellent example of the technique. It carries one of the symbols of Chalchihuitlicue, Lady Precious Green, who was thought to manifest herself in whirlpools

organizations were run. So they kept themselves to themselves and celebrated the worship of their own special god Yacatecuhtli, which means Lord Nose. They had special ceremonies, which included tying their staves together each evening wherever they made camp, and making an offering before them. They considered that the staff, which helped them on the road, was a fitting symbol of their god. When they had a successful venture and returned home with fine things from other districts, they would hold a festival in one of their houses. The houses were usually poor on the outside, but within there were many fine goods from other lands. The ceremonies often broke the puritanical Aztec traditions, and there were dances with naked girls, either members of the merchants' families or slave girls who had been bought in markets among other tribes where Aztec ideas of behaviour were not so important.

When going on a trading expedition, the merchants came to a market place and announced the intention of their journey. They might then be joined by considerable numbers of men who welcomed the chance of adventure. Each member of the expedition had to carry up to 80 pounds on his back as he walked from town to town, across rivers, up mountains, sometimes reaching almost to the treeless zone of snow, sometimes diving deep in ravines in the coastal area, which brought them into the humid tropical jungles. The rewards were a visit to strange lands, the sight of the fine things found in different parts of the country, and the enjoyment of exchanging news in the various market places which were visited.

Merchant societies had an added importance as carriers of information from town to town. Not the least important part was military information quietly remembered and reported to the Aztec war leaders. Sometimes, in fact, merchants were hired to cause trouble in areas where the Aztec army intended to conduct a military campaign. Merchants would find some way of insulting the local chief, so that he would attack their convoy. This would give an excuse for the Aztec armies to march in a pretended effort to make sure the ways of the traders throughout the country were safe.

In the pages of *Codex Mendoza* there is a record of the tribute paid by the various towns of Mexico to Montezuma and the Aztecs. From this, we can learn of the rough distribution of the main commodities: fine woven cloths from the north and west; purpura shells from the Pacific coast, which were used to make dyes; cochineal from the mountains; cacao beans from the south; gold from the south-east and the far north of the country; fine wood carvings from the hill country where the forests produced better timber; and a great deal of cotton, brought in as tribute from the warm southern plains. The amounts gathered were remarkable, many towns contributed anything from 6,000 to 10,000 blankets. Others would provide many thousands of necklaces of jade beads. The gold-bearing areas gave their contributions in quills taken from eagles' wings, each quill being filled with gold dust to a specified volume. There was no method of weighing materials in ancient Mexico, and all trade was done in volume.

The market place was one of the most important parts of any town. Merchants from other cities brought goods for sale and exchange, and all the producers of food, cloth or pottery would bring their products, and meet to barter and exchange goods. The market was very carefully organized, and an area was set aside for each class of merchandise. People circulated exchanging pieces of news and gossip so that the market place was also the main source of information. Expensive goods on the market might be bought with little axe-blades of copper, which were made by the Chinantecs of

north-western Mexico, or with jade beads or gold dust.

The merchants submitted to a certain amount of state control. Every town had a market supervisor, and in Tenochtitlan he was one of the four highest chiefs of the state. The Aztecs considered it important that their nation should have a reputation for fair dealings. It was, therefore, made possible for anyone who felt themselves cheated to appeal to the market controller. The case would be examined on the spot by a group of advisers who tried to determine the truth of the allegations. If a trader were found guilty of cheating by selling goods with a false description or by giving unfair quantities, he was summarily punished. In most cases this simply meant confiscation of his goods, but in serious matters it was considered right for the market controller to order that the trader be mutilated or even executed. A false accuser could be similarly punished, so people had to be circumspect in these

temple .
palace .
ball court .

Left: The more sophisticated Aztec pottery was reserved for noblemen and priests. The fine eating bowl, top, is decorated with the symbol of the wind serpent. It stands with two cups used for drinking pulque, and these carry a symbol representing the eye of the Earth Monster. The dish, bottom, was almost certainly used ceremonially and is painted to show a jaguar in the centre, with the symbol of fire around him

Below : Panel from the Codex Fejervary-Mayer *showing Yacatecuhtli, Lord Nose, the patron god of the merchants. His large red nose makes him easily identifiable, and he is carrying the symbol of the cross-roads with merchants' footprints on them. The merchant on the right carries the characteristic fan and staff, while on his back is a cargo of precious quetzal birds*

matters. In the more important towns markets were always open, but in lesser places there would be markets only once in 20 days, at the beginning of the various religious festivals, when festival mementoes and images of the gods were on sale. The latter usually took the form of little clay figurines, a few inches high, which were taken back and kept in a special niche in the home, where they were regarded as protective spirits for the household.

The volume of trade within the Mexican economy was immense. This is partly because of the wide-ranging journeys of the Pochteca, but also because there were demands for certain special goods; for instance, beautifully made and embroidered garments were often sold by women who had acquired a reputation for the quality of their work. Most Aztec women made their own pottery, but there were special cases in which high-grade pottery was made, beautiful in form, and

painted in orange and black, or sometimes with a full polychrome treatment like the paintings in the codices. The designs painted on these vessels may originally have been sketched out by scribes attached to the temples.

There was a strong trade in feathers imported from the tropics. These were arranged in the market in little bundles of selected colours, and they were used in featherwork. They were placed on sheets of prepared amatl, or fig bark paper, pasted down, and the edges were trimmed to precise lines. The feathers were treated with such exactness that a piece of feather work could very well be mistaken for a painting. They were made up into the faces of shields, and war shirts for great warriors. Carefully polished beads and plaques of turquoise and jade, all of which had been through the workshops of trained lapidaries attached to the temples, were also on sale. They took this precious material and engraved designs on the surface, usually with sharp, pointed quartz crystals. They could also polish the stones into relief figures, working entirely with pieces of wood or cane dipped into quartz sand. The making of such small sacred objects was considered a religious task, and they were of such immense value that they were collected by great noblemen.

The city on the lake

The way of the trader was the way of all travel in ancient Mexico. The tracks over which the goods were carried from town to town were also the roads which could be followed by armies. The tracks therefore had to be kept in reasonable condition for the sandalled feet of the great trains of carriers. Though this did not involve paving them, it did include a certain amount of drainage and the provision of ropes along the way to assist people up and down steep slopes. In a few places, steps were cut in the sides of cliffs and short stretches of pathway were hewn around great rocks. On the whole, however, the tracks had been formed to serve the local trade and ran reasonably straight from one city to another, meandering only when ascents were too steep to be negotiated directly. The tracks crossed mountains and rivers, negotiated deserts or found ways through tropical forests, and though they were in no sense good roads, they played a vital part in the history of the country.

A major problem for the Aztecs lay in communication with their great city of Tenochtitlan. Once they had established themselves there, and had become powerful enough to occupy portions of the shore of the lake, they had set to work building great causeways, mostly of the soft and lightweight volcanic stone they knew as Tezontli, which was also used for buildings in the city. These causeways were meant to take troops to the mainland, as well as bring in supplies of food. Firm ground was found across the lake bed and foundations were laid. The finished causeways were elevated some six feet above the level of the waters, and they were deliberately interrupted at several points. This was partly in order to allow the waters of the lake to flow freely during storms and floods, but it was also a defensive measure. Each gap was normally bridged by great baulks of timber, hewn mostly from cedar and cypress trees. In times of danger these timbers were simply rolled back onto the part of the causeway nearest the city and a gap was left, which could not be crossed. It is true that one of Cortes' company, Alvarado, made a famous leap across one of these gaps, but he used his lance as a vaulting pole, something with which no Mexican had ever been equipped.

The city itself was traversed by canals in every direction. Each canal had a paved pathway beside it, so although most Aztec contacts around the lake were by

Right: The legends surrounding the foundation of the city on the lake, Tenochtitlan, tell of Huitzilopochtli, the Aztec patron god, and his promise that when the Aztecs reached the right place to build they would see an eagle perched on a great cactus and bearing a serpent in its claw. This stone carving depicts the eagle, and symbols show the date of the city's foundation which was AD 1325 in the western calendar

canoe, there was still room for foot traffic. Normally the Aztecs went from place to place at a steady trot covering great distances without exhaustion, at a speed of around five or six miles an hour. On the mainland, paved roads were hardly necessary, and at the end of the causeways the country tracks began.

Under the conditions of Tenochtitlan it is not surprising that there were many small figurines of the water goddess. She seems to have had a little niche in many houses where offerings were made to her. They not only thought of her as a provider of fertility and food, but also as a dangerous force of destruction. They had good reasons for this, because great storms occasionally lashed the lake into a fury, and there was danger of flooding in parts of the city. This could cause houses to be undermined and fall into the canals. There were also occasional seismic disturbances. During Montezuma's reign alone there were two occasions in which the lake appeared to boil, the water became whitish and great waves formed, blown by no wind, which threatened the safety of the city. Naturally, these were thought of as omens of coming troubles, and showed the power of the water goddess. She was beautiful and young, the wife of the rain god, but she had to be treated with great care to forestall her sudden, temperamental outbursts.

Aztecs working the fields beyond the shores of the lake often built themselves temporary huts of wood and cane, with leaf-thatched roofs. In the city, however, nearly every building was made from Tezontli. It was easy to cut this soft, volcanic rock to useful sizes and to pile the blocks neatly into walls. The walls were held together by cement made from burnt limestone. The usual house consisted of a single room about 15 feet long and 10 feet wide. It had a square doorway, about five feet high, in the middle of one wall. The door was capped by a wooden lintel which was often painted a bright red. The roof of the house was usually made of

wood, beams and planks, covered by a layer of brushwood. This was sufficient to keep out the usual rains, partly because it was slightly tilted to one side. In the better houses the roofs were supported by beams and covered with layers of cement. It was common for the householders to spend part of the day, at least in the warm, dry season, on the roof of the house, under cotton awnings which shaded them from the sun.

Farther towards the centre of the city, houses were owned by the more important citizens. These were usually built as quadrangles, one storey high, in which each side contained four or five rooms, each room being the size of a normal house. In the middle of the courtyard there was usually a pool, and pleasant flowering plants were grown there for the delight of the inhabitants. The walls were usually plastered with a fine, white cement, polished so thoroughly that it would glisten in the sun. Frescoes in bright colours were painted around the doorways. The whole inner part of the city was well-built and brilliant to look at, with small paved squares which served as markets.

The heart of the city was centred on the gigantic pyramid of the rain and war gods. The courtyard of the temple contained several beautifully painted buildings dedicated to many different deities, including one which housed the gods of the conquered tribes. In another part of the courtyard was the Tzompantli, a rack of skulls which were threaded on canes thrust through the temples. These were the skulls of 10,000 enemy warriors slain in sacrifices at the temple. Around the whole temple enclosure there was a wall called the Coatepantli, the 'serpent banners', carved with representations of rattlesnakes in honour of the Earth Mother. It must have been a beautiful sight in its own strange way, but it was totally destroyed, and nothing remains except a few fragments of the foundations.

Around this wall was a broad passageway, and this was flanked by the palaces of past Great Speakers of the nation. These palaces were carefully preserved, and within them the treasures of the original owners were kept in good condition and displayed occasionally to visitors from other tribes, so that they should gain a proper understanding of the glory and importance of the Aztecs. The palace of the last Great Speaker, Montezuma, was apparently very large. After entering by the gateway and passing a courtyard, the visitor came to further courtyards surrounded by low buildings, all brilliantly painted. In the centre was a solid

Above left: Reconstructed priest's house at Teotihuacan. This type of lintel and post construction was common in ancient Mexican cities and would have been continued in Tenochtitlan. Houses for priests and nobles in Tenochtitlan faced inwards, like this one, onto a central courtyard

Above: Rattlesnakes return again and again as motifs in Aztec art because of their close connections with the earth. The wall surrounding the great temple enclosure of Tenochtitlan was called the Coatepantli, the 'serpent banners', and was carved with representations of rattlesnakes

masonry plinth ascended by a staircase, on the top of which stood the house of Montezuma himself. It contained a series of richly decorated rooms, with carved beams of cedar, decorated with gold leaf. The floors were covered with beautiful skins and finely woven rugs, and the walls were plastered and painted.

The visitor came wearing the simplest clothes and only a coarse cactus-fibre cloak to cover him. He had to approach the Great Speaker crawling and bowing his head to the ground. When he looked up he was supposed to squat, and, at first, shield his eyes so that they should not be blinded by the glory of his host.

Though the Great Speaker was glorified, it was always customary that he should listen to the advice of his council. The council consisted of the high priest, the governor of the market, the supreme army commander, and a representative of the judges whose court was just to one side of the palace. This distribution of power was quite effective, and, if the Aztecs had wished, they could have extended this simple system to co-ordinate their entire empire into a single political unit. Basically, of course, the presence of the Great Speaker indicated that the government was not only chosen by the tribal council, but also by the gods, in particular, the great Huitzilopochtli, patron of the Aztecs. This dual dependence of the Aztecs upon social organization and the gods was absolutely characteristic of their whole civilization. Beyond it they could make no advance and they can have seen no reason for change.

The view from the top of the great central pyramid, 170 feet above the city of Tenochtitlan, must have been breathtaking. All around lay low houses, many brilliantly painted, and the waters of the lake beyond would have been thronged with canoes. The fields lay on the farther shores, coloured bright green by growing maize plants or the deeper, brownish-green of the areas lying fallow. All around, in the distance, were mountains, covered by dark forests of pines, except for the great volcanoes, Ixtaccihuatl and Popocatepetl. The brilliant, white snowcaps were never traversed by the Mexican Indians, as they were considered too holy for humans, and were dedicated to Tlaloc and his wife as the places from which weather came. All around them, near the tree line, there were small temples from which the smoke of burning rubber continually rose.

This was the centre of a great empire. Tenochtitlan, at its height, housed nearly a million inhabitants and brought together all the arts and crafts of a great civilization, although the technological levels were not far removed from those of neolithic farmers. It is obviously surprising that this should be so, and it can only be compared with the early cities of Mesopotamia, as they were some 4,000 years earlier. Despite apparent stagnation, however, a great deal of knowledge and wisdom was accrued by the priests and rulers of this strange world.

Astrology and the Priesthood

Above: Tonatiuh, the sun god, with a symbol representing an earthquake on his back. According to astrological reckonings an earthquake would finally end the world and, with it, the present sun

Left: The Aztec day ran from sunset to sunset, and the contrast of night and day formed the basis of astrological reckoning. On this page from Codex Cospi, *offerings are being made by the sun god, top, and by the god of darkness, below. The sun god stands before a temple in which an eagle is enthroned, while the god of darkness stands before a temple inhabited by the rational owl, a symbol of utter destruction*

From what we know of the Aztec religious system it is quite clear that the priests had done a great deal of work over the centuries, attempting to correlate several religious beliefs. The differences between them may have been partly historical, but in many cases they were tribal. The many tribes revered many gods as their patrons, so that there must have been some confusion. It is clear that the surviving codices were dedicated to various gods and were the result of joining up different traditions. It also becomes clear, however, that a system had evolved which came to be considered as something unchanging and eternal. The painters of the codices envisaged a universe ordered by a great company of gods under the sovereignty of the great Ometecuhtli who was beyond all worlds, wiser than all gods, and the ultimate source of all life, beauty and success.

Fate and the stars

The most important group of specialists were the astronomers, who had the use of simple observatories in their work. One way of assuring the position of a given star was to take a visual bearing on another object, such as a mountain peak or a distant temple tower. If the exact bearing of this point was taken it was quite easy to mark the movement of the stars through the sky. In the Aztec codices many priests are shown making observations with the help of a cross-shaped piece of wood, balanced on two corners on a sighting block held at arm's length. This provided a sighting point from which the movement of a star or a planet could be noted in relation to the horizon. There are no existing star maps to give exact information, but it is certain that the passage of time was carefully noted, that certain constellations were named and that all the visible planets were observed, their movements computed, and predictions of their future positions made.

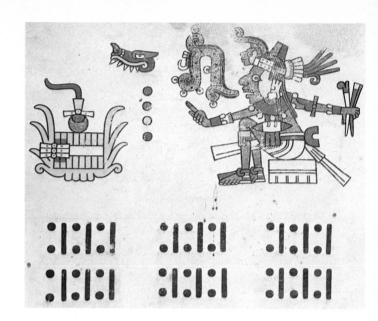

Right: Astronomical information was accurately noted by the ancient Mexicans in their sculpture and in the codices. In this panel from the Codex Fejervary-Mayer *a minor planetary deity is shown with bars and dots, the numerical system used by the Aztecs, each bar representing five units and each dot one. When added together, these numbers probably represent the synodic period of the planet, that is the number of days between its occupation of the same relative position in the sky*

Opposite page: On this Aztec relief Tonatiuh, the sun god, is shown as a diving eagle setting below the horizon. He is surrounded by skulls from the underworld which he enters every night. The stern face of the god has a stone sacrificial knife as a tongue

The most important of all the planets was, of course, Venus. Its dual identity as Quetzalcoatl, the Morning Star, and Xolotl, the Evening Star, was theologically important, but it is quite clear that the Aztec astronomers realized that they were dealing with a single planet. Venus as a planet was under the tutelage of a very dangerous god named Tlauixcalpantecuhtli, which means Lord of the House of Dawn. This god is shown armed with throwing spears, which on certain days he casts at various social orders: at women, at warriors, and at farmers. These days were therefore regarded as dangerous ones in which people should make an offering to the planet Venus, and, if possible, abstain from their normal activities. Failure in life was easily ascribed to the dart of this god.

The little planet Mercury was also observed. He was the young prince, Piltzintecuhtli, and appears in several of the picture writings, notably in the beautiful *Codex Borbonicus*, now in Paris. Here he is shown at several of the seasonal festivals, indulging in widely different activities, thus reflecting the nature of the little planet, which appears either as a morning or evening object for only a comparatively short time—because its period of revolution around the sun is very short. He seems to be a spirit of changeability, and of frustrated attempts to ascend. All the other planets can be identified, and some of their synodic periods, that is the periods between their appearance at the same place among the stars, are included in numerical calculations. But it appears that although they represented gods, they were by no means as important in the regular life of the Aztecs as Venus and Mercury.

The changing position of the fixed stars in the night sky was obviously important for astrology. The stars were divided up into constellations, and those which we know about appear to have been roughly the same as the constellations adopted in the European astrological tradition. Aquarius was a sign associated with the water

god Tlaloc, and Scorpio was also the sign of the scorpion to the Mexicans. As has already been said, the Pleiades marked the beginning of every 52 year cycle. In fact, most of the major groups of stars had significance.

Most people had little opportunity for observing the stars, since going out at night, although people always used torchlight, was considered very dangerous, and people remained indoors between the hours of sunset and sunrise whenever possible. Only candidates for priesthood braved the terrors of the night, and went out on their own to perform special missions. Many years of training and the acceptance of the rigours of ceremonial fasting and privation were necessary to become an adept astrologer.

Among the many priestly duties of the Great Speaker, was that of making observations of the stars, from his palace roof at sunrise, at midnight, and at sunset. He was thus kept aware of the general condition of state affairs. Montezuma, for example, who was the last Aztec Great Speaker, was a fully trained priest as well as a national leader, so he was aware that the points of origin and direction of movement of shooting stars were of great importance. He also knew that the appearance of a 'star serpent', a comet, was of great historical significance. For Montezuma, astrological predictions were of great importance, since although he was personally, as both priest and ruler, dedicated to the god Quetzalcoatl, the fate of his nation was dependent upon its patron Huitzilopochtli. Thus, in the one man there must have been a state of constant anxiety because of the inherent dissension between the two gods.

An important function of priestly dignitaries was to forecast events. They calculated the relative positions of planets and star clusters and in this way reached decisions which might have been appreciated by astrologers in modern Europe. But the system of time counting that they used was very different indeed. It was based on the Tonalpouhalli, the book of fate, which is depicted in several of the surviving codices. This system does not contain any long periods of domination by one particular spirit: the 13 gods of the day take their turns on each successive day of the 13-day period, and the 9 lords of the night rule over each of 9 successive nights in order. There was no period of continuous rule under any one constellation or during the appearance of any one planet. The higher priests did, in fact, make calculations from the positions of planets and the stars, but these were also conditioned by reference to the book of fate. A few years ago the author worked with two friends on an imaginary horoscope, one using the standard European procedure, the other an Indian method, both of which were then compared with the Aztec version. Each worked separately, with the same theoretical date, and, for no obvious reason at all, the answers were remarkably similar.

Each group of thirteen days, over which constantly changing lords of the day ruled, was included as a block of time in the codices, ruled over as a whole by a duality of gods, who are depicted with significant events surrounding them. These systems for dealing with the sequence of time, however, were used mainly by priests. For practical, everyday affairs, the year was made up of 20 groups, each of 18 days, with 5 extra days at the end. Each of these 20-day groups had its patron deity as guide and protector. From this very slight account, one can appreciate the great complexity of the system and the amount of time the priests must have spent learning the inner meaning of each possible combination of time periods. It was important to them since they firmly believed that the patterns achieved by the various time counts reflected events in the life of the people, subjected as always to the fates shown in the Tonalpouhalli.

Above: This unique temple was built by the Totonacs at Tajin. There are exactly 365 niches in its sides, one for each day of the year. While it is obviously connected with the calendar, the exact purpose of the temple remains a mystery. It seems probable, however, that each niche contained pottery or wooden images of the god dominating the particular day represented, and offerings were probably made before each niche in turn

The priesthood

Education was available to all who wished. Every boy went through military training from the age of about 13 until he was ready to begin army service. Both boys and girls were welcome at the temple schools, where the boys trained as priests and the girls as temple helpers. The trainees suffered considerably: they were not allowed to sleep on mats, but only on the hard stone floor of the halls of learning; they wore little clothing, and were taken out at night to gather various insects, including scorpions, which were later incinerated to make the black body paint of the priests. This was a dangerous occupation, and if a child was stung, it was taken as a sign that he had been rejected by the gods, so he was cast out, to return to everyday life. Gradually the children learned to recite long stories of the deities, and to assist at sacrificial ceremonies. They had to observe

all the details of rigorous fasting, and only on rare occasions were they allowed any spiced food or fruit, so that for at least half the year they lived on only three *tortillas* and a bowl of water a day.

Training in these schools was highly specialized. Some of the boys became the painters of sacred books and the designers of sculpture. Some of the girls became healers and studied the excellent Aztec pharmacopeia. Treatment mainly consisted of herbs and the use of the sweat bath. According to the Spaniards, who had practical experience, this was usually quite successful. In fact, many of the herbal plants used by the Aztecs have found a place in modern medical practice, although in a very much more refined state. The young men also learned how to dress wounds and bandage fractures so that healing was natural and did not lead to deformity. There is so much information about these skills, that they must have embodied centuries of experience.

It was also important for the healer to know the appropriate chants to the gods, since it was recognized that everything that happened to a person was part of the fate willed by the gods in charge of the period when it happened. Offerings therefore had to be made, and prayers recited, and this was probably of considerable psychological importance in the promotion of cures. Only in very serious cases was the divination by casting of maize grains used, for fear that a bad prognostication would hasten the end of the patient. Illustrations in Aztec documents, particularly in the drawings made for Father Sahagún's great work, give drawings of the medical herbs, but also show patients being examined and conducted to the sweat baths. It was usual to have the sick person shown with tears running from their eyes, to express the misery caused by illness.

All Aztec priests were expected to be conversant with the general outlines of astrology, but there were many grades and many functions. A priest was selected, not because of his social rank outside the temple, but because of his willingness to undergo the austerities demanded, and his ability to carry out the duties of his office. Every day he must make sacrifices of his own blood to the gods, not only from his ears like the common people, but also by piercing his tongue to offer blood. On all the greater ceremonial occasions he cut the calves of his legs or pierced them with cactus spines, so as to have blood to offer to the gods. His foreskin was pierced by cactus thorns, and torn until his penis was surrounded by a fringe of strips of flesh from which blood could easily be taken. Naturally, this implied, and was meant to assure, a celibate priesthood. The importance of virginity, both for the priests and among the women helpers of the temple, was absolute.

The priest was normally painted with a black, magical ointment from head to foot. On great occasions, his face, at least, was painted with the marks of the god whose festival was being celebrated. Even when going into war the priest would wear his magic black paint. His hair was never cut and it was stained with splashes of blood from human sacrifices. Nor was it ever washed, so these strange, black figures were crowned with untidy masses of coiling, clotted locks, which apparently smelt horribly, and were infested with insects. Yet, in spite of these horrors, the priest, dressed in his long, black gown with little white crosses on it, was felt to be somebody holy and powerful.

It seems that most priests were philosophically disposed, though some were certainly numbered among those unfortunate persons, important in all religions, who are seized upon by the gods and driven into a trance, during which they may be forced into a series of wild actions while the gods speak through their mouths. These prophets were sometimes brought in

Above: Relief from Santa Lucia Cozumahualpa showing an astrologer-priest holding the paddle-like staff used to fix a point for astronomical observation. He is wearing a double-headed serpent, one of the many symbols of Tlaloc

from outside the normal priestly school, because they were people who were considered to have been chosen by the gods themselves. The régime of priestly life involved much fasting. Long periods of living on only three *tortillas* and a bowl of water a day resulted in an austere and dedicated personality. Only after many years had a priest acquired the necessary ritual holiness to perform sacrifices for his gods. It seems that he can have had no feeling, except that his work should be good and that a heart should be removed by a single slash of his stone knife. This was the highest office, and the sacrificing priest was respected by all, because of his close relationship with the tribal god.

There must have been occasional clashes between personal wishes and the demands of religion. It was believed that anyone breaking the strict code would bring misfortune to his family and tribe, so that any known transgression was likely to attract punishment from society. Conversely, it was realized that people were subject to fate, thus the commission of a theological crime against the gods was not considered so much wrong, but more as a misfortune caused by the day on which the person had been born. This did not, however, prevent punishment itself, since the punishment was also part of this system of inevitability.

The gods could not change their nature, neither could they relent or forgive, except on one occasion. The offering of sacrifices particularly of personal pain, and deprivation of pleasure, might well ease the fate attached to the person, but it could not be totally extirpated. There was no room at all in this system for simple forgiveness or atonement.

Once in every lifetime, however, it was possible to receive forgiveness for all previous sins. This was a function of the priest of the Lady Tlazolteotl, the Eater of Filth. This goddess was one aspect of the Moon, and was the power behind all witchcraft and magic in the Aztec world. In her third phase this moon goddess was also a goddess of purification, and was supposed to accept all the filth of sin into herself, thus taking it away from the penitent. But once confession had been made before the priest and the images of the goddess and Quetzalcoatl, there was no further chance. Most people, therefore, delayed the confession of their sinfulness until they were ageing.

When forgiveness was sought the penitent was stripped quite naked, and he then had to enumerate all the evil deeds of his life. Any action of cowardice in the army, or refusal to obey the gods, or neglect of any sacrifice, or any sexual deviation from the established norm was carefully detailed. Offerings were made before the gods and in their name the priest announced absolution. After this the penitent was constrained to go away and sin no more. As has been said, sin was not counted particularly as wrong doing, but as a consequence of fate, yet, in the context of this confessional, it was clear that fate could be adjusted, and that the accumulation of debt within the personality could be cut away. This gave a new chance of living according to the rules, and so assured a happy death.

There was no room for the deviant philosopher in the custom of the Aztecs, or in any of the nations in Central America. It was essential that all worshippers conformed entirely to the official beliefs. Even those individuals who were at the very peak of society might propound important doctrines which favoured one god or another, but it was unheard of that they should deny the system. There was no harsh materialist to 'pervert' the youth of the nation like Socrates in Greek culture, and no great teacher to denigrate the gods as did Plato.

Nezahualcoytl, ruler of Tezcoco on the eastern shores of the lake, was said to be one of the greatest of Mexican philosophers. He had warned that the sacrifice of 20,000 men at the dedication of the great temple was not acceptable to the gods, who would have normally demanded only 20. He realized that terror in the name of religion was only weakening the respect that was paid to the dominating power. He also propounded a belief in the power of one special god, so that Aztec accounts deluded later Spanish writers into the belief that Nezahualcoytl was a monotheist. When we read the name of his god, however, we find it was Tloque Nahuaque. This was simply another name for the terrible Tezcatlipoca, so this philosopher-king should really be credited with an idea very palatable to Aztec ears, that the god Tezcatlipoca was the greatest of all gods, as important or more important than Ometecuhtli, the divine power from beyond the earth.

It becomes clear, then, that Nezahualcoytl was formally in line with the ideas of the military ruling classes of Mexico, and not really an innovator. It is quite understandable that the concept of such a militaristic god should have been understood by the Spanish conquerors. Like so many other European Christians, they thought of themselves as the witnesses of an ancient Hebrew deity, Jehovah, whose destructive punishments of mankind are detailed in the Old Testament. However, the Aztecs were conformists within their own religion, and since they had no temples to Ometecuhtli, they did not particularly worry about the very mild aberration on the part of the Lord of Tezcoco.

All Aztec citizens had to take part in the ritual worship of the gods. They had to attend the temple ceremony that occurred once every 20 days, make the appropriate offerings, dance the appropriate dances, and wear the appropriate face paint. Unless a person was seriously ill and the illness was known to all his neighbours, the disgrace of not attending one of these highly emotional religious outbursts would be very great. Conformity to the tribal pattern was an essential part of all Aztec life and religion, which, of course, put great power in the hands of the priesthood.

Above: Life-size Totonac clay figure of a priestly dignitary. Many of the rulers and noblemen of Mexican societies undertook training as priests since it was essential that they understood the astrological basis of their fate and that of their nation. The highest office a priest could hold would be as the sacrificial executioner in the main temple, but astronomer-priests were constantly computing the cyclic movements of the stars and planets, and their calendrical significance. They were always consulted before great ventures were undertaken

The Earthly Confrontation

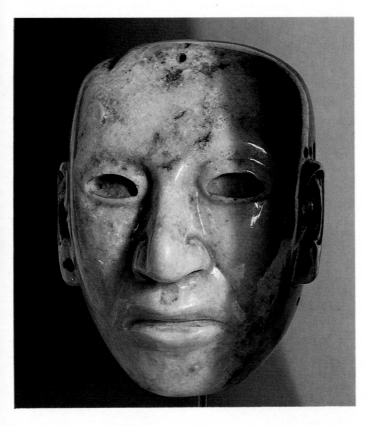

Above: The wealth and glory of one of the ancient world's greatest cities, Tenochtitlan, is suggested by this beautiful jade head. The hole in the forehead indicates that it was used simply as a pendant by a nobleman or high-priest. By 1508 the Aztec hegemony extended over the entire land of Anahuac and tribute was brought into Tenochtitlan from all directions, including precious stones, gold, cocoa, rubber and many raw materials

Left: In the early sixteenth century reports came to Tenochtitlan from the east of great canoes with white wings, carrying strange men dressed in stone. Eventually, in 1519, Hernando Cortes landed near Cempoalla on the Caribbean coast in charge of an expedition from Cuba

The driving power behind the Aztec dominion over Mexico was the belief in their god, Blue Hummingbird, one of the aspects of the great demiurge, Tezcatlipoca. He was the power of magic, the mysterious Smoking Mirror in which visions were seen. To him the Aztecs attributed the glories of their conquests, and for him the great temple towered into the sky. Blood was constantly offered in his temple at the top of the pyramid. In the dark interior priests poured bowls of human hearts in front of his image glowering in the gloom. No Aztec would have denied that this god had led the tribe from poverty to power, yet they all knew very well that this great 'shadow' was also a being of unrelenting cruelty.

The last Great Speaker of the Aztecs, Montezuma, knew better than most that the god of the Aztecs was unreliable. In the earlier years of his reign the Aztecs had suffered terrible disasters. An army of 16,000 warriors had been destroyed in western Mexico when they had been caught up in a violent mountain storm and hurricane winds. Some were crushed, most were drowned, and few survivors returned to Tenochtitlan. Nevertheless, other wars were started, and they brought in streams of prisoners to be sacrificed, so that the tribe could become rich, and its terrible patron could be appeased.

In the midst of the great city, Montezuma was splendid in his isolation. He had at last, by 1508, brought about the fulfilment of the ancient promise that the god had made to his people. The Aztecs ruled all of Anahuac, from Atlantic to Pacific. In his day, the city was splendidly colourful, its markets were constantly busy, its people were well dressed, and its warriors were feared throughout the land. Because of his earlier training as a priest, Montezuma was well aware of the mutability of fate. Everyday at sunset, midnight and dawn, he observed the sky from his palace roof to divine the course of events. To him, the signs in the sky marked the marching of fate, and his policies were dictated by his reliance on the priestly training which had made him an adept of great wisdom. The position of the starry symbols of the gods in the night sky, their relation to the planets, the appearance of comets and meteors, all gave him information to help him amplify the indications in the Tonalpouhalli, the sacred book of fate.

There was, however, a central dichotomy in the spiritual world of Montezuma. He was properly elected to the leadership of the Aztec people, and was therefore dedicated to their patron god, Huitzilo-pochtli. Their fate and welfare, he realized, depended upon the devotion the nation showed through him to this mighty power. But Montezuma himself was born on a day sacred to the Morning Star, Quetzalcoatl. He was thus directly involved in the strange conflict between the two deities. From our modern standpoint Tezcatlipoca can be seen as a projection of the 'shadow' side of human nature, and Quetzalcoatl as the fully conscious intelligence of mankind. In Mexican myth-ology these two gods were part of a great complexity of divinities. The inevitability of their conflict is as clear from the legends in the painted books as it might well be to a psycho-analyst today. Montezuma was well aware that this strain was present, and he must also have believed, possibly because of his own descent from the Quetzalcoatls of the Toltecs, that one day the power of Quetzalcoatl would be restored. The possibility of this return would occur in a year called Ce Acatl (one, arrow-reed), which was the name of Quetzalcoatl as Morning Star, and on the day Chiconaui Ehecatl (nine, wind) which was the birthdate of the first Quetzalcoatl. This combination occurred every 52 years, and it was expected only once in the lifetime of Montezuma, in the spring of the year 1519.

Naturally the mind of the Great Speaker was focused on this important date which had so much personal meaning to him because of his Toltec lineage. He was well aware of the struggle between Tezcatlipoca and Quetzalcoatl when Tollan had fallen into anarchy some five centuries earlier. No doubt he had more detailed and more important documents than the *Codex Vindobonensis* which alone remains for us. His oc-casional pilgrimages to the sad ruins of the city must have emphasized the duality he felt within himself. He was at once both the ruler who had revived the glories of the Toltec Empire, and the leader of the Aztec nation whose patron god was the terrible being responsible for the fall of the Toltecs.

In the year 1508 there had been a solar phenomenon which the Great Speaker must have seen. A tiny black speck moved slowly and steadily across the face of the sun. It was not the usual sun spot, which might have been confused with it, and Montezuma was well aware that it was the planet Venus in transit. This was a rare event and the jade figure of Quetzalcoatl wearing the sun as his neck ornament, which is now in the collection of the British Museum, was probably a memorial of it. Such a rare event, occurring only once in nearly 300 years, must have been seen as a first warning of the events to come.

Stories came to Mexico a few years later of a strange phenomenon. From the eastern coasts, in the Maya country, and soon after from the coasts of the Totonac lands ruled by Montezuma, came tales of strange, giant canoes with wings. From them had come men clad in stone who killed by pointing sticks at people. In many places these strange, black-bearded creatures had landed and bartered with the people. Then they sailed away northwards. Montezuma felt that this was the second appearance of the deformed people whom Quetzal-coatl had taken away with him on his retreat from Mexico. This was, in fact, the trading voyage of the Spanish adventurers Solis and Pinzon. Their map was

Above: This beautiful featherwork shield was almost certainly the ceremonial parade shield of Montezuma's great uncle, Ahuitzotl, who preceded Montezuma as Great Speaker. His name means the Water Beast, which is the creature depicted by the featherwork. The outlines are marked in gold, and show that the beast is holding a stone sacrificial knife in its jaws. This shield may have come into Cortes' possession as a gift from Montezuma, but it seems more likely that this is part of the treasure discovered by the Spaniards which sparked their greed and led to the final débâcle

Left: Double-headed serpent encrusted with turquoise and red and white shell, which probably formed part of the treasure sent to Cortes by Montezuma, who believed Cortes to be the returning god Quetzalcoatl. This serpent was one of the symbols of Tlaloc, and was worn as a pendant by a high priest

published in Spain by Peter Martyr de Angleria, though the sailing directions had been falsified. It is probable that gossip had spread back to Cuba where young Hernando Cortes was running a small plantation, worked by Carib slaves.

At this period Cortes did not know his fate, but was hoping one day to make his fortune in some profitable foray among the islands. He was a gentleman of high birth but low fortune. Physically, he was short, and well-groomed, though a fall from a young lady's window had broken his leg and left him permanently lame. His complexion was a soft brown, and his black hair and neat beard set off luminous, dominating eyes. That he would one day be regarded as the symbol of a deity returning to Mexico can never have entered his dreams, though he was fated to live that part.

The third figure in the approaching drama was the Princess Malinalli of Painalla. She had been born on the

day Ce Malinalli (one, grass of sorrow), under special symbols in the sky which indicated that she would, throughout her life, be opposed to the terrible war god of her Aztec people. To protect the child her mother showed a false daughter to the priests, a baby girl which had been born dead to one of her slaves, and sent her own child to the Maya people in Yucatan. Later on she was to be known to the Spaniards, who could not pronounce her name, as Marina, and because she was of noble birth they called her Doña Marina. The fate of millions hung on the lives of Montezuma, Cortes and Doña Marina, for it was through them that the battle between the gods was to be enacted.

Strange signs continued to be reported in Mexico, and Montezuma must have become uneasy. He continued to lead his people wisely, distributing maize when the harvest was bad, and giving clothing once a year for the poor of his city. The great temple dedicated to Smoking Mirror, and Tlaloc the rain god, was constantly active. Prisoners were taken there and slain to the glory of the gods of Mexico. Great parades and festive dances continued as usual, but Montezuma must have remained constantly overshadowed by his coming fate. A cruel and sudden blow befell him when his aunt, Princess Butterfly, was thought to have died. She had in fact fallen into a cataleptic trance, and three days later some children playing in the palace saw the 'dead' lady sitting up. She asked them to fetch her nephew; when Montezuma came to her, delighted at the astonishing news of her recovery, he found her lamenting. She then told him of the vision she had experienced during her trance. She spoke of men clothed in black stone and riding upon hornless deer. They came to Anahuac, and then marched, burning and hunting people down, before coming to Tenochtitlan itself. There they were gathered with Montezuma, and she had seen him lying dead among them. She saw the whole city in flames, while the leader of the horrible, white-faced creatures sat enthroned among the ruins of the city.

Montezuma knew that the vision had been sent as a warning, to show that the god Quetzalcoatl was destined to destroy the people of Tezcatlipoca. Nothing could avert it, yet he eventually came to hope, after he had spent many hours in meditation and consultation with the soothsayers, that a middle way might be found. Perhaps he felt that he could placate the approaching god of the Morning Star, so that the Aztecs would not be wholly destroyed. It is recorded, however, that, from this time, the Great Speaker of the Aztecs became withdrawn and uncommunicative. He was evidently sad at heart, and even though his armies brought many victims for Huitzilopochtli there was a shadow at the back of his mind.

More strange happenings were reported. Strange beings apparently materialized, and gave messages of doom before they disappeared. People came rushing in terror to the palace, declaring that they had met apparitions which had warned them that the great city in the lake would be destroyed. A fiery serpent had appeared in the heavens, and it was visible in the same place in the sky for more than a year.

For Hernando Cortes, too, a time of great change was near. Rumours of a land across the Caribbean sea were rife, and it was reported to be a land full of gold, and so populous that there would be an unending supply of slaves. Slaves were an added attraction, for the Caribs too often committed suicide rather than work for the cruel white men. The Governor of Cuba planned an expedition, but it was delayed, and eventually it was handed over to Hernando Cortes to command. Originally it was planned simply as a reconnaisance, to trade and to discover whether there was really a treasury of gold ready for the taking. There were some Spaniards who were religious men, and saw a chance of converting the heathen to the true faith. A trio of

friars went with the expedition, and, as the Spaniards were all Catholics—none more devout than Hernando Cortes—the expedition assumed a little of the character of a crusade.

The first landfall was the Isla de las Mugeres, a limestone islet just off the coast of Yucatan. Here the expedition discovered a temple, of which the pillars were grotesque figures of women. Before it were the remains of human sacrifices, but they found no local population. Then they sailed along the coast of the heavily forested peninsula, and finally discovered that the stories of a rich and well-populated land were true. In some of the Maya cities they visited they were welcomed as traders, while in others they were attacked, and in return they killed hundreds of Indian warriors. It was a grim progress: there can be no doubt that the news travelled to the Mexican towns and reached Montezuma in his palace. The significance of these stories cannot have escaped him, for the year Ce Acatl was soon to begin.

At one of the coastal towns Cortes and his men met a Spanish novice-priest who had been shipwrecked six years previously. He had been befriended by a local Maya chief, and, having learnt their language, was able to act as interpreter. The local townspeople fêted the distinguished strangers, bringing bales of cloth, little golden bells, good food, and a bevy of 18 nubile girls. Among these girls was the Princess Malinalli, who was given to a spaniard called Alonso Puertocarrero. She was now nearly 18 years of age, old enough to know her past, and, perhaps, to appreciate her destiny, so that she was more interested in gaining the ear of Cortes himself. It appears that she too thought that he might be Quetzalcoatl. She talked with the interpreter, and in three weeks she had learned enough Spanish to talk with the Spaniards. She already spoke Maya, of course, and had learned the Nahuatl language of her mother's people. It was not long before Cortes took her as his interpreter, and it seems that he soon fell in love with her.

In the spring of 1519, messengers arrived in Tenochtitlan with the news that strange, winged boats and ugly, bearded men were moving through the Maya coastal waters and were approaching the coasts of the Totonacs now under Aztec control. Montezuma was horrified. He thought of handing over the country to the approaching god, then of resisting. He retired to meditate on the destruction that fate must bring to him. During meditation he must have decided to remain a servant of Tezcatlipoca, who had always protected the Aztecs, and to temporize with the invaders. It was to be a carefully timed game in which the invaders were to be attacked only when the astrological conditions demanded. He was, however, ready from the first to accept the representatives of Quetzalcoatl, who was, after all, one of his ancestors.

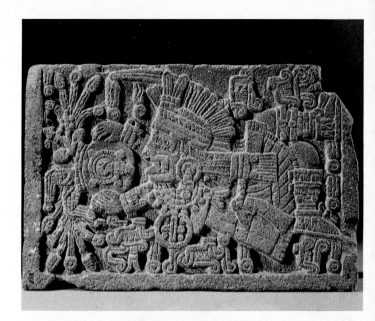

Above: Stone box which once contained the ashes of the Great Speaker Ahuitzotl, represented on the inside of the box, below, by the Water Beast surrounded by water. The base of the box, top, shows one of the messengers of Tlaloc overturning a bowl of rain

Above right: The planet Venus, Tlauixcalpantecuhtli, attacked various social orders with darts during certain periods in its cycle. This page from the Codex Cospi *illustrates a period when it is attacking ocelot warriors, represented by the ocelot on the right. The spear from the god has passed through the ocelot's heart*

On the afternoon of Maundy Thursday, April 20, 1519, the ships came to the coast of Mexico near Cempoalla. Indian visitors to the ships paddled out in great fear, but were received with kindness by Cortes. Messengers were sent running to Tenochtitlan. Cortes did not land on that day, but the next day brought its fated events. For the Spaniards, it was the solemn occasion of Good Friday and those who could, dressed in black. For Montezuma it was the birthday of Quetzalcoatl in the year of Quetzalcoatl. He must now have felt quite sure that his fate was determined.

Montezuma had been secretly preparing suitable gifts to mark this arrival, and his jewellers made ornaments of jade and gold to welcome Quetzalcoatl. He took some of the equipment of the gods from the great temple in Tenochtitlan, including the serpent mask of Quetzalcoatl, and the black mask of Huitzilopochtli as patron of dark magic. Some books were included,

of which the most important was the one containing the story of Quetzalcoatl, now in Vienna. These gifts were taken to the coast by messengers. Quetzalcoatl was to be welcomed, though the black mask in the package might have been intended to test him, for Quetzalcoatl would thus be faced with his rival. Cortes, however, just put it on one side with the other gifts, intending to send this treasure to the King of Spain as an earnest of the greater gifts which would come when Mexico was conquered.

As soon as Hernando Cortes had landed near Cempoalla, he was drawn by an Aztec scribe and the picture was sent rapidly to Montezuma. In this drawing it was not difficult for the Aztecs to see the expected features of the returning god: the strange, pale face; small, black beard; black painted limbs (his hose and gauntlets), and a hat shaped like the Huaxtec hat worn by Quetzalcoatl. On his breast, set in gold, was a white shell, like

Above: The dramatic skyline of the ruins of Cempoalla.
Here Cortes formed his first headquarters and here, too,
he fought and defeated the forces brought by Narvaez from
Cuba, thus making sure of his own supremacy among
the Spaniards entering Mexico

the wind-jewel of the god. The resemblance was perfect. But the god acted strangely. He had made friends with the conquered Totonacs, and had captured and later released the nobleman who had been collecting tribute for the Aztecs. In short, he was persuading the tribe to stop paying tribute to the Aztecs.

Uncertainty changed to fear. The strangers carried long arquebuses which could kill at a distance, and were riding deer with no horns. Such things had never been seen in Mexico before. Their priests accepted offerings not of humans but of fruit and flowers, just as had been the case in the days of Quetzalcoatl. They hired long trains of porters to carry their goods and marched inland towards Cholula. Montezuma was persuaded by his commanders and the priests that this was a good time to attack the invaders and strike for the honour of their gods. Plans were made during meetings of nobles from Cholula and the Aztecs.

The Spaniards entered the city. The beautiful Doña Marina was much in evidence among the houses of the noblemen, talking and listening. She became suspicious of a trap because she had noticed warriors watching from house tops, so she went to visit an old noblewoman and heard from her of the plot to destroy Cortes in the streets of the town. She returned to Cortes with a warning, and he sent scouts who were then attacked. Having found a good excuse, he commanded a general assault. Against tremendous odds, the Spanish destroyed the forces of Cholula, while an Aztec army, advancing through the maize fields, was too late and had to watch helplessly while the Spanish stormed the great complex of pyramid temples dedicated to Quetzalcoatl. This must have been a grim blow to Montezuma, for Cholula was a great shrine to the Toltec God-King.

The failure of the Aztecs was all the more terrible because, for the first time, Cortes had been assisted by tribal levies of Tlaxcalan warriors. He had been forced to battle with the Tlaxcalans, had defeated them, and they had now joined him. This was very bad news for the Aztecs, because they had deliberately not conquered the Tlaxcalans so that they could, from time to time, be raided for sacrificial victims. The Tlaxcalans were wildly excited when the Aztec power in Cholula was smashed and they saw a chance of marching against Tenochtitlan itself. As might have been foreseen by anybody but dedicated theocratic militarists, the Aztecs were hated by their subject peoples, and the isolated Tlaxcalans felt free to vent their fury in honour of their tribal god Camaxtli, the Deer God.

After these battles the Spaniards rested a little, stitched up their wounds, polished their rusting armour, and made themselves new sandals. Already the campaign had become a battle of endurance. There could be no turning back, since Cortes had already burnt the ships so that the fittings could be used in the campaign, and as a precaution against desertion.

The march continued from Cholula, ascending to the plateau and on towards the dark pine forests and the snowy peaks of the volcanoes. The Aztecs decided to use magic, and a group of nobles with a few warriors arrived as an embassy of peace to Cortes. They brought splendid gifts and food for the divine visitor. As usual Doña Marina translated, and she noticed that the leaders spoke the colloquial Nahuatl and not the very elegant and refined version of the language spoken by her family, and by all Aztec nobles. The Spaniards seized them, and, under the strappado, they confessed that the meat they had brought was from human sacrifices offered to Blue Hummingbird. It was taken and burnt, and the crippled magicians were sent back to Tenochtitlan. Marina had realized the perils involved in this magic. She believed that if Quetzalcoatl-Cortes had eaten offerings which had been made to Tezcatlipoca, he would have either vanished as matter in the presence of anti-matter, or else have been stricken dead with the sign of the Aztec war god upon him, the terrible symbol of the single turkey claw. When Montezuma heard the news, he realized that the gods had met and that Huitzilopochtli had been defeated.

One test remained: the Aztecs were determined to discover whether this new Quetzalcoatl could recognize Montezuma, and so another embassy was prepared. The Spaniards, meanwhile, continued their march, though they must have been weary, and most had been wounded in the many battles they had faced. They marched onwards through pine forests, and into the belt of scrub which led to the col, at great altitude, between the two great volcanoes, Smoking Rock (Popocatepetl) and the White Lady (Ixtaccihuatl). It was windswept, barren and snow-strewn, but they persevered. The Tlaxcalans were terrified of the mountain gods, but they still followed, carrying the baggage. Breathing is difficult at those altitudes, but by now the Spaniards were acclimatized and they marched slowly and steadily on. From a ridge of mountains they caught their first glimpse of Tenochtitlan. There, far below in the valley of cultivated fields, lay a huge lake, and in the midst of it, shining in the sun, was a great city painted in white and red. The tall pyramid temples towered in two groups and ascending columns of smoke could just be seen. The Spaniards reported later that it was like a vision of magic. They must have been both entranced and afraid, for they now realized that they were marching to confront a great empire and a king renowned for the barbarity of his sacrifices and the valour of his armies.

Soon a fine procession approached carrying gifts, and, in the midst, a nobleman impersonated the monarch. But again Marina saved the Spaniards by noticing that this man spoke in reply to a question, whereas Aztec etiquette demanded that the Great Speaker should only reply through interpreters, and never speak directly. So the imposture was uncovered. This time, a messenger was sent back to Montezuma protesting friendship and expressing a hope of meeting.

The march continued, and the villages and small towns on the trail were crowded with astonished onlookers who had never seen a horse before, and who believed Cortes to be a returning god, so they sang songs of welcome. The army crossed the level fields and came, with some trepidation, to the causeway across the lake leading to the city. In front of them they saw the Aztec army advancing, but there was no going back. They had polished their equipment the previous night, so that they presented a splendid appearance, soldiers and knights in shining armour followed Tlaxcalans in war-paint and feathers, bearing burdens into the city of their hated persecutors.

The two processions met, Cortes dismounted and he stepped forward with Marina. A golden litter halted in front of them, and noblemen knelt as they placed magnificent cloths for the occupant to descend. A small, thin man with a slight beard stepped out. His sandals were of gold, his loin-cloth and cloak were of turquoise blue. His crown was made of turquoise and his armlets and necklaces were of gold and jade. Green quetzal feathers were set in a fan at the top of his head-dress. People fell on their faces before him as he advanced to meet Cortes. His interpreter recited the words of welcome, and Marina translated, giving properly humble welcome to the great war leader of nations. Cortes bowed and the two leaders clasped hands, each accepting the other with equal respect. Then Cortes rode beside the golden litter as they passed over the causeway and its bridges. The lake was thronged with spectators in canoes, watching the procession enter the crowded city. The Tlaxcalans, however, were forced to camp outside the city, since Montezuma thought them too

primitive to enter, and feared that they might turn on the citizens without warning.

The Spaniards were housed in the palace built by Montezuma's revered father, Axayacatl, about 40 years previously. They were astonished by its size and luxury, but they must have begun to worry about the consequences of their successful entry into the city. The date was November 8, 1519.

It seemed for some time that there would be peace in Mexico. Cortes and Montezuma achieved a very real respect for one another which was close to friendship. The Spaniards were made welcome and found that the Mexicans would help them with food and servants. They even persuaded the Aztecs to give them gold, but Cortes was a strict disciplinarian and his men were kept busy drilling or mounting guard. Montezuma horrified him by showing him the temple with its dreadful images and bloodstained altars. But then he gave Cortes a chapel in which a Madonna was placed so that Father Olmedo could say Mass.

Unfortunately, some of the Spanish soldiers saw a blocked-up wall in the palace, prised it open, and found a room filled with incalculable riches in gold and jade. It was a matter for immediate action. Cortes could not risk a mutiny, and the soldiers demanded more plunder. With all possible politeness, the Great Speaker was persuaded that he would be murdered if he remained in his own palace. A virtual prisoner, he went to stay with Cortes, giving away the treasure and pretending that it was of little moment. He knew that fate was still being worked out and that he was trapped by the spirit of the 'shadow', the patron of his people. Even when several of the great nobles of Tezcoco and some of the Aztecs implored permission to assassinate Cortes, Montezuma refused. Yet he was always hopeful, and early in May, 1520, he received a message from the coast. More Spanish ships had arrived, and they had imprisoned the followers of Cortes. This might present a possibility of escape,

and he waited some days before informing Cortes. As usual Doña Marina translated, and Cortes immediately guessed that the Governor of Cuba, Velasquez, was behind this attack. He was forced to divide his forces. The less experienced stayed in Tenochtitlan under the command of Alvarado, whose golden hair was so bright that the Aztecs called him Tonatiuh, the sun. Montezuma was well treated once more, and he promised to remain within Tenochtitlan. He probably thought it best that Spaniard should kill Spaniard, for by now he must have realized that his captors were not divine, though he must still have seen the struggle as a matter of fate.

So Cortes went to the coast and met the far superior forces led by Narvaez. There was a conference, and much bribery with Mexican gold. Then several of the visitors were invited to join Cortes to share the gold of Mexico. A battle followed, in which Narvaez was severely wounded, and Cortes won the day. He then persuaded most of the new invaders to join him, and thereby trebled the number of horsemen in his forces. During the banquet that followed a runner came from Alvarado to say that the Aztecs were in revolt, and the position of the troops in Tenochtitlan was desperate. Later, the truth came out, and Cortes discovered that while the midsummer festival of the war god was being celebrated, the great warriors of Mexico had come to dance in full war dress before the temple. Alvarado had been frightened that an attack was coming, so he had struck first, slaying the flower of Aztec nobility, and many of the priests.

Cortes returned to Tenochtitlan as fast as he could, but this time, instead of welcome, he found a silent city. Stones were piled beside the bridges, ready for war. No sound was made and there were no boats on the lake. When they entered the palace the Spaniards were

Above: Craftsmanship in Mexico did not die out with the Spanish invasion. Like all strong cultures, it endured and adapted, as is shown by this powder horn. It was made by Mexican craftsmen from cowhorn, a material entirely new to them, and includes Aztec motifs as well as the carving of a Spanish ship shown here complete with a look-out perched on the central mast

Above left: Sculptured rocks and figures which once formed part of Montezuma's summer palace. It was quite normal for the Great Speaker and other nobles to move out of the city in the long hot summers, and to build palaces in the surrounding hills. This palace, like the imperial city, suffered complete destruction

quietly welcomed by Montezuma. Cortes knew, however, that the Aztec nobles who visited the Great Speaker might take messages to the rebels, so Montezuma was seized. Although Cortes tried to prevent it, Montezuma was tortured to ascertain where gold was hidden. Ominous noises of gathering crowds reached the Spaniards in the palace, and soon stones began to fly. There was nothing to do but to bring Montezuma to the walls so that he could be seen by his people. The Great Speaker signed for them to be silent, and a deadly hush fell upon them. Montezuma probably knew what was to follow. From the crowd a voice called that he was no longer the Great Speaker, and had been replaced. He stood quite still, and then three stones flew through the air. His crown was knocked off and fell, scattering turquoise on the ground. His head was gashed, he knelt and then fell. That was the signal for a hail of missiles against the palace. Fires were started, and a gate broken, but the Spaniards eventually repulsed the crowd. Montezuma was taken down to a basement, where some say the Spaniards murdered him. Others suggest that he refused treatment and died stoically after tearing off any bandages the Spaniards tried to place on his wounds. Whatever happened, it is certain that Montezuma died on June 30, 1520.

Meanwhile, there had been fierce street fighting, and the Aztecs continued to stone the Spaniards and Tlaxcalans. The battle surged, and the Spanish broke through to storm the great temple and cast down the images of the gods. The Spaniards no longer had Montezuma as their protector, however, and Cuitlahuac, the new war chief, was a brave fighter. A few Spanish were taken and sacrificed, as well as many Tlaxcalans, but they were not enough to save the image of the dreadful war god.

There was nothing for the Spanish to do but find a way out of Tenochtitlan, and one moonless night they began the retreat. A long procession left, with two of the daughters of Montezuma under the protection of Cortes. All went well for a while, but then, as they halted where a bridge had been broken down, a war whistle was sounded and the attack began. Warriors dragged Spaniards and Tlaxcalans from the causeway and drowned them in the muddy lake. The fighting was fierce, and when morning came few survivors had reached the mainland. Two thirds of the Spanish army had been destroyed. Cortes, Marina and the band of survivors sat down, exhausted, under a cypress tree.

To their surprise the Aztecs did not attack at once. There was a delay of four days. Then, at Otumba, the refugees met a great Aztec army. Cortes attacked first and cut his way through to the litter on which the Aztec war chief was carried. The commander was thrown to the ground, and the armies melted away. Every Spaniard was wounded, but most eventually returned with the surviving Tlaxcalans to their homeland where the

Council of Tlaxcala met. They so hated the Aztecs that they chose to continue the war despite their losses.

A great revolt of subject peoples was now under way, and Aztec power was on the wane. Montezuma was no longer there to mediate, and the Aztecs now had to face alone the magic of Quetzalcoatl. Now they saw it as wielded by black-robed friars who worshipped a god who had died on a cross. The struggle was no longer equal for the followers of Smoking Mirror, and they were simply fighting heroically in a final self-sacrifice.

Cuitlahuac was, however, conquered by another ally of the Spaniards—the 'red death'. A soldier in the army of Narvaez had been a carrier of smallpox. In the epidemic of 1520–21 a fifth of the population of Mexico died. After Cuitlahuac was cremated, the Aztec council elected Cuauhtemoc as leader of the nation. He was a brilliant and brave young man, but however valiantly he fought there was no hope of success.

The Spaniards gradually conquered all the towns on the shores around the lake and cut off all Aztec lines of communication by building sailing boats with small cannon which destroyed the Aztec canoes. After five months of continuous fighting the blockade was complete. The Spaniards attacked but they were driven back, and the Aztecs refused to parley or to surrender.

Much against his will, Cortes was forced to advance by destroying the city, house by house. The Aztecs were starving, but they fought on until the invaders reached the palaces and the square in front of the great temple. Then a canoe, filled with feathered warriors, was seen leaving the city and a Spanish boat set off in pursuit. Shortly afterwards Don Juan Jaramillo led in the brave Cuauhtemoc as a prisoner, and the war was over. The temple at the top of the great pyramid caught fire and some Aztecs later said that they had seen Huitzilopochtli fly away in a thunder cloud.

Above left: Turquoise and shell encrusted mask of Quetzalcoatl, the Feathered Serpent. The face is formed by the intertwining of a blue serpent and a green serpent, which coil around the eyes and mouth with their plumed tails covering the forehead

Above: Mask of Tezcatlipoca, the Smoking Mirror, formed of turquoise with pyrites eyes and built over a human skull. The two great gods represented on these pages can be seen as two sides of the human mind: Quetzalcoatl being conscious intelligence, and Tezcatlipoca the unconscious 'shadow'. The fate of their nation was seen by the Aztecs to hang on the confrontation between these two gods

The few Aztec survivors, including three daughters of Montezuma, left the city. The place was a terrible ruin populated by the rotting corpses of those who had died of smallpox, starvation and war. For months nobody went to it. Cortes held a council and it was decided that no other place could ever be the capital of New Spain. So the old city of Tenochtitlan was levelled to the ground. Even the ruins of the old temple were blown up with gunpowder and a cathedral built on the site. But the date remembered in Mexico is the Feast of Saint Hypolito, on August 15, 1521, on which Cuauhtemoc surrendered in the ruins of Tenochtitlan.

That was the day of the triumph of Quetzalcoatl, but it was a new Quetzalcoatl. The Christian ethos, which came near to the code of conduct advocated by the first Quetzalcoatl, replaced the past of sacrifice and terror. Amid bloodshed and tragedy, the 'Breath of Life' had returned to form Mexico anew.

Glossary

Anahuac Name meaning the 'land between the waters', that is ancient Mexico from the Guatemalan mountains in the south to the deserts in the north, excluding the Yucatan peninsula.

Aztecs Warlike Mexican tribe who came to establish an empire dominating the whole of Mexico from their centre of Tenochtitlan. Defeated and decimated by the Spanish conquerors in the early sixteenth century. (*c.* AD 1325 to the fall of Mexico)

Chalchihuitlicue Goddess whose name can be translated as Lady Precious Green or Lady Precious Jewel. Water goddess and consort to Tlaloc, the rain god.

Coatlicue Earth Mother venerated as the basis of all fertility and growth and associated with numerous lesser fertility deities.

Codices Magical painted books of ancient Mexico in which history and religious teachings were recorded. In the absence of a written language, these paintings convey precise symbolic meanings.

Ehecatl Lord of the Winds: the aspect of the god Quetzalcoatl associated with fertility.

Great Speaker English rendering of Uetlatoani, the title given to the supreme ruler of the Aztec empire, who ruled with the aid of a council of four elders and was elected to office by the noblemen from among their own ranks.

Huitzilopochtli One of the many aspects of the god Tezcatlipoca; the name is translated as 'Blue Hummingbird on the left'. This deity was the particular patron of the Aztecs whose central temple was dedicated to Huitzilopochtli and Tlaloc.

Maya Tribe inhabiting the Yucatan whose great civilization appears to have grown and faded independently of events in Mexico. (*c.* 200 BC to *c.* AD 900, then neo-Maya until AD 1550)

Mixtecs Mexican tribe inhabiting southern Mexico. Among the last to be dominated by the Aztecs, and renowned for their craftsmanship. (*c.* AD 700 to the fall of Mexico)

Montezuma Great Speaker of the Aztec empire whose attempts at appeasing Cortes and the Spanish finally led to humiliation and death at the hands of his own people. (AD 1467 to 1520)

Mictlantecihuatl Lord of the Dead; Aztec deity ruling the underworld, Mictlan.

Nahuatl Language of the Toltecs and Aztecs, related to languages spoken by North American tribes.

Olmecs Tribe with the earliest developed culture in Mexico, centred on La Venta. Their origins and downfall remain a mystery. (*c.* 1200 BC to *c.* 600 BC)

Ometecuhtli Creator and highest deity in the Aztec pantheon inhabiting the region around the Pole Star.

Pipiles Minor proto-Toltec culture centred on Santa Lucia Cozumahualpa in Guatemala. (*c.* 100 BC to *c.* AD 650)

Quetzalcoatl Name given to the ruler of the Toltecs, after their first priest-king, who became deified and identified with Venus as Morning Star. Among the many symbols connected with the god was the Feathered Serpent. Aztec mythology later identified Quetzalcoatl as a banished, diminished god who would one day return.

Tenochtitlan The great city built by the Aztecs on islands at the centre of the Lake of the Moon. The city was completely obliterated during the Spanish conquest, but Mexico City now occupies the same site.

Teotihuacan City on the Mexican plateau in which a great and highly influential culture flourished until the seventh century. It was the forerunner of the Toltec/Aztec cultures.

Tezcatlipoca Central deity in the Aztec pantheon, one of whose aspects was the patron of the Aztec nation. This dreadful god was symbolized by the Smoking Mirror and was the foremost recipient of human sacrifice.

Tlaloc Rain god; among the most ancient of the Mexican gods, and highly venerated as a bringer of fertility.

Toltecs Mexican tribe who created an empire based on Tollan, now called Tula, in Hidalgo. Their gods and mythology formed the basis of Aztec belief and Aztec noblemen claimed descent from the Toltecs and married Toltec princesses. (*c.* AD 750 to *c.* 990)

Totonacs Mexican tribe inhabiting eastern coastal regions. (*c.* 100 BC to the fall of Mexico)

Xolotl The god associated with Quetzalcoatl as his sinister twin; Venus as Evening Star.

Zapotecs Mexican tribe inhabiting southern coastal regions. (*c.* 100 BC to the fall of Mexico)

Chronology

BC	
2000	Village cultures developing throughout southern Mexico particularly on the Mexican plateau
1000	Olmec culture spreading from mountains to coast in south-eastern Mexico
	Full development of Olmec culture in southern Vera Cruz (south-eastern Mexico)
800	
600	Olmec culture nearing its end
400	
	Monte Alban 1 culture in Oaxaca (south-western Mexico) begins with Olmec artistic influences
200	Development of Teotihuacano culture on Mexican plateau
	Beginnings of Maya culture in Yucatan
AD	Beginnings of Zapotec culture on southern coast and Totonac on eastern coast
	Pipiles on Pacific coast of Guatemala
	Teotihuacan a flourishing city
	Pyramid at Cholula begun. Flourishing cultures on Gulf coast of Mexico
200	
	Beginnings of Maya inscriptions. Teotihuacanos rule at Kaminaljuyu in Guatemala
	Teotihuacan dominates all central Mexico

400	Maya art highly developed
	Apogee of Pipil art on Pacific coast of Guatemala
	Transit of Venus in 580 recorded at Santa Lucia Cozumahualpa by Pipiles
600	Pipiles on the move into Mexico from south
	Fall and destruction of Teotihuacan
	Solar eclipse with Venus visible in 750. This marks the death of the first Quetzalcoatl and the beginning of the sequence of Toltec Kings
800	
	Mysterious collapse of Maya culture; all great cities abandoned without destruction
	Civil war among the Toltecs. Tollan destroyed
1000	
	Interregnum after fall of Tollan in which the country is anarchic, and Chichimeca peoples wander from the north among the ancient towns
1325	Foundation of Aztec capital at Tenochtitlan
1487	Consecration of the great temple in Tenochtitlan
1492	Christopher Columbus discovers the West Indies
1502	Montezuma elected as Great Speaker of the Aztecs
1504	Cortes leaves Spain for the West Indies
1508	Transit of Venus seen in Mexico
1514	Spanish adventurers visit eastern Mexico briefly
1518	Cortes commissioned to take an expedition to Mexico
1519	Cortes lands in Mexico
1520	Death of Montezuma, last Great Speaker of the Aztecs
1521	Fall of Tenochtitlan to the Spaniards

Bibliography

Early sources (Publication dates are of latest edition)

HISTORICAL CODICES

Codex Bodley, Bodleian Library, Oxford.

Codex Egerton 2895, British Museum, London.

Codex Magliabecciano, Biblioteca Medicea-Laurenziana, Florence.

Codex Mendoza, Bodleian Library, Oxford.

Codex Selden, Bodleian Library, Oxford.

Codex Telleriano Remensis, Bibliothèque Nationale, Paris.

Codex Vaticanus A (Rios), Biblioteca Apostolica Vaticana, Vatican City State.

Codex Vindobonensis Mexic. I, Österreichische National-bibliothek, Vienna.

Codex Zouche-Nuttall, British Museum, London.

Codices Becker I and II, Museum für Völkerkunde, Vienna.

Petitions of the Indians of Tepetlaoztoc, British Museum, London.

Selden Roll, Bodleian Library, Oxford.

RELIGIOUS CODICES

Codex Borgia, Biblioteca Apostolica Vaticana, Vatican City State.

Codex Cospiano, Biblioteca Universitaria, Bologna.

Codex Fejervary-Mayer, Liverpool City Museum, Liverpool.

Codex Laud, Bodleian Library, Oxford.

Codex Vaticanus 3773, Biblioteca Apostolica Vaticana, Vatican City State.

Acosta, Joseph de, *The Natural and Moral History of the Indies*, Hakluyt Society, London 1880.

Alva Ixtililxôchitl, Fernando de, *Obras históricas*, 2 volumes, Mexico 1891 and 1892.

Alvarado Tezozomoc, Fernando de, *Crónica mexicayotl*, Mexico 1949.

Cervantes de Salazar, Francisco, *Crónica de la Nueve España*, Madrid 1914.

Díaz del Castillo, Bernal, *The True History of the Conquest of New Spain*, 5 volumes, Hakluyt Society, London 1908–16. *The Conquest of New Spain*, Penguin Books, Harmondsworth 1963.

Duran, Diego, *The Aztecs. The history of the Indies of New Spain*, Cassell, London 1964.

Sahagún, Bernardino de, *Historia general de las cosas de Nueve España*, 4 volumes, Mexico 1956.

More recent works

Anton, Ferdinand, *Ancient Mexican Art*, Thames and Hudson, London 1969.

Burland, Cottie Arthur, *Magic Books from Mexico*, Penguin Books, Harmondsworth 1953.
The Gods of Mexico, Eyre and Spottiswoode, London 1967; Putnam, New York 1967.
Montezuma: Lord of the Aztecs, Weidenfeld and Nicolson, London 1972; Putnam, New York 1973.

Caso, Alfonso, *The Aztecs, people of the sun*, University of Oklahoma Press, Norman 1970.

Joyce, Thomas Athol, *Mexican Archaeology*, Macmillan and Co. and Philip Lee Warner, London 1912; Hacker, New York 1969.

León-Portilla, Miguel, *The Broken Spears. The Aztec account of the conquest of Mexico*, Constable, London 1962; Beacon Press, Boston 1962.

Nicholson, Irene, *Firefly in the night*, Faber and Faber, London 1959.

Peterson, Frederick A., *Ancient Mexico*, George Allen and Unwin, London 1959; Putnam, New York 1962.

Prescott, William Hickling, *The Conquest of Mexico*, 2 volumes, Chatto and Windus, London 1922.
History of the Conquest of Mexico, abridged, ed. Gardiner, C. Harvey, University of Chicago Press, Chicago 1966.

Soustelle, Jacques, *Daily life among the Aztecs*, Macmillan, New York 1962.
The Daily Life of the Aztecs on the Eve of the Spanish Conquest, Stanford University Press, Stanford 1961; Penguin Books, Harmondsworth 1964.

Vaillant, George Clapp, *The Aztecs of Mexico*, revised by Vaillant, Suzannah B., Penguin Books, Harmondsworth and New York 1965.

Index